What Shall We Tell the Kids?

What Shall We Tell the Kids?

BY
Bennett Olshaker, M.D.

To T.A.O. and our kids
Mark   Robert   Jonathan

Copyright © 1971 by Bennett Olshaker

All rights reserved, including the right of reproduction in whole or in part in any form. Published in the United States by Arbor House Publishing Co., Inc., New York, and simultaneously in Canada by Nelson, Foster & Scott, Ltd.

Library of Congress Catalog Card Number: 71-169923
ISBN 0-87795-022-9
Manufactured in the United States of America

CONTENTS

Preface   13

Chapter I   The Family

Parents and the Blame for Children's Problems   18
   "Is it always the parent's fault?"
The Job of a Father   21
   "I saw you. You were shaking him."
The Job of a Mother   26
   "Because we have no uterus."
Affluence   29
   "You don't appreciate anything."
The Family: An Emotional Laboratory   31
   "I hate you. I wish you'd go kill yourself."
Authority   34
   "The Constitution guarantees me the right of life, liberty, and the pursuit of happiness."
Parental Consistency   35
   "My husband is so strict I have to make up for it."
Physical Punishment   37
   "You must not have spared the belt on your son."
Moral Teaching   40
   "So the money belongs to you."

Chapter II   Doctors, Hospitals, and Operations

Introduction   46
Visits to the Doctor   47
   "Why did they take out so much of my blood?"

Contents

Psychiatry	51
"Do you think I'm crazy?"	
Watching Our Language	54
"I've got a disease and I want to go home."	
Going to the Hospital	56
"What's going to happen when I go to the hospital?"	
Should Parents Stay?	59
"They usually behave better when the parents aren't here."	
Scheduling Elective Surgery	62
"Does it have to be done now?"	
Fears of Younger Children	63
"Will they take my wee-wee off?"	
Tonsillectomy and Adenoidectomy	67
"What are tonsils? What's an operation?"	
Hernia Repair	69
"What did they take out of me?"	
Broken Bones and How They Heal	71
"Will my leg still be there?"	
Emotional Reactions to Injury	76
"I blew it. I blew the whole summer."	
Hospitalization of a Parent	78
"Is she coming back?"	
The Fatally Ill Child	81
"It makes me sad to see him suffering."	

Chapter III Education

College Entrance	86
"We didn't get into the college of our choice."	
Payment for Grades	89
"Johnny, you make me feel very proud and happy."	
Allowing an Option to Fail	92
"What kind of mother would I be if I did that?"	
Teachers	95
"I certainly hope you're as bright as he is."	
School Phobia	98
"I'm afraid I'll throw up in class."	

Contents 9

Chapter IV Handicapped Children

The Parent's Feelings ... 104
   "I wished he had died at birth."
The Child's Feelings ... 106
   "What happened to your leg?"
The Sibling's Feelings ... 109
   "I wish they would take my foot off."
School Problems ... 111
   "I will not have that child with the hook in my school."
Should Retarded Children Be Kept at Home? ... 113
   "Put him in an institution as soon as possible."
Minimal Brain Dysfunction and Hyperactivity ... 115
   "With a motor running all the time and no brakes."
The Mildly Handicapped Child ... 119
   "Kids keep calling me the 'Jolly Green Giant.'"

Chapter V Death

Explaining Death and Burial ... 124
   "I looked on every cloud."
Funerals ... 126
   "May I go to the funeral?"
Permitting Grief ... 128
   "Big men don't cry."
Fear of Abandonment ... 131
   "Who will take care of me?"
Children's Guilt ... 133
   "It's my fault she died."
Death of an Abusive Father ... 135
   "His wife and kids will be better off."
The Child's Anger ... 136
   "I hate God!"
Children Should Be Children ... 138
   "I'm the man of the house now."
Disguised Unhappiness ... 140
   "He wasn't even sad."
Suicide ... 142
   "How did Mom die?"

Chapter VI Adoption

Telling the Child   146
"*Why didn't you tell me I was adopted?*"
Telling the Adopted Child about Conception   149
"*Where did I come from?*"
The Angry Adopted Child   151
"*You're not my real mother.*"
The Adopted Child's Fear of Abandonment   153
"*Who will take care of me if anything happens to you?*"
Heredity, Environment, and the Adopted Child   155
"*Yes, he's my boy.*"

Chapter VII Separation and Divorce

Introduction   160
Telling Children About Divorce   161
"*I must have been a bad boy.*"
Don't Ask the Children   164
"*Whom do you want to live with?*"
Too-Friendly Parents   166
"*If you're so happy together, why are you getting a divorce?*"
Constancy of Visitation   167
"*Dad, you used to come every week. What happened?*"
Meaningful Visits   169
"*Dad doesn't pay much attention to us.*"
To Win Is To Lose   172
"*I went bowling with Dad and I beat him again.*"
Caught in the Middle   175
"*What has your mother been doing?*"
Be Truthful but Not Vindictive   179
"*You go ask your father.*"
The Need for Security   182
"*I'll have to send you to live with your father.*"
The Child and Sexual Impulses   185
"*You kissed Mother like a little lover.*"
Mother's Confidante   187
"*You can tell me your troubles, Mother.*"
Divorced Parent and the Grandparents   189
"*Who's the boss of me anyhow?*"

Contents

Chapter VIII Remarriage

The Angry Stepchild 194
"You're not my mother."
Being a Parent 196
"He's your child, you tell him what to do."
Deciding To Remarry 198
"Do you want me to marry him?"
Competition with Stepparent 200
"You love him more than you do me, don't you?"
Half-Siblings 202
"I wish I had two mommys like Lynn."
Children's Need for Stability 204
"It's our turn to have them for Christmas."

Chapter IX Sex

Elementary Sex Education 208
"Does he push it in?"
Adolescent Development 211
"She'll probably be menstruating soon. Is this normal?"
The New Sexual Freedom 214
"Is there anything wrong with me because I'm not doing it?"
Homosexuality 219
"Do you want them to think you're a sissy?"

Chapter X Modern Problems: From Pot to TV to Mixed Marriages

Television 226
"Buy three sets and put one in every room."
Diet and Exercise 230
"I wish I could get some and take it home to my parents."
Drugs 233
"Promise us you won't try pot."
Marriage 236
"I thought he would change."
Religion 238
"He could choose for himself when he got older."

12 Contents

Prejudice — 241
"Why don't people like blacks?"
Toy Guns — 242
"Bang, you're dead."

A Parting Thought — 244

Index — 245

PREFACE

KIDS ARE CURIOUS. They wonder about things and often worry about events that they don't understand.

Sometimes, they ask questions of their parents; at other times, and for various reasons, they are reluctant to ask. They may sense that the adults will be uncomfortable about answering. When this happens, children may seek answers from their peers—and frequently acquire misinformation. Or from their own imaginations they may supply answers that can be quite bizarre.

Parents and substitute parents are the important people to a child. They are the ones who should attempt to supply adequate information that will satisfy the child's curiosity.

How Do We Tell Our Kids?

Parents are a child's primary teachers. The infant's education begins at birth, and as he progresses through stages of emotional development he receives many messages from his parents and, later, from other significant adults.

In the beginning, the baby receives information through nonverbal communication; for example, through touch and the way in which he is held. Later, words become important, not only the actual words that he hears, but the feelings that he senses go with the words.

We also tell a child a great deal, usually much more than we realize, by our actions and the example we set. Children quickly note any discrepancy between what we tell them and what we actually do.

Why Shall We Tell the Kids?

In order to make the best progress in the development of his personality, the child needs a relatively stable environment with understanding parents who set limits for him and provide him with the opportunity to experiment with his feelings and to satisfy his curiosity. In such a setting the youngster will find ways and means of coping with the emotional problems that all of us experience throughout life.

Fate sometimes acts to make things difficult, however. Certain events add significantly to the problems that children must face. Separation and divorce, remarriage, the hospitalization or death of a parent or child, and handicaps of one kind or another can present special difficulties for children.

Many of these events also cause trouble for the adults involved, but children are especially vulnerable as they are in the midst of developmental processes. Youngsters are often the innocent victims. Usually they would not choose to have things the way they are, yet there is little they can do to change the situation. What we tell children in these circumstances becomes extremely important if we hope to minimize the ill effects of potentially traumatic situations.

But what we tell our youngsters about less "serious" things —matters of education and family relationships, for example —is also of significance. Through our words and actions we help them shape their attitudes toward life, and hopefully prevent problems before they arise.

When Shall We Tell the Kids?

Parents often say in regard to a particular aspect of living, "My children never asked any questions about that." What actually may have happened is that the child did ask and was told, "I'll tell you later." When "later" never comes, the child assumes that he should not have asked the question in the first place. And when the parent no longer is questioned, he tends to forget the time when the child did ask.

It is desirable, therefore, to try to answer questions as close as possible to the time that they are asked. In the same way, if important events are occurring, we should tell children about them as close to their occurrence as we possibly can. If we do not have the information necessary to answer the child's inquiry, we should tell him that we will try to find out as soon as we can. And we should remember to tell him as soon as we do find out.

WHAT SHALL WE TELL THE KIDS?

Before giving information to a child about a particular problem or event, it is wise to try and learn from him what he thinks about the subject and what misconceptions he may have. We should listen to our child and try to hear what he is saying. In this way we have an opportunity to correct any erroneous information he may have acquired or can help straighten out any misconceptions he may have developed in his own mind.

We should tell children the truth. Parents at times feel that it is better to lie so that the children will be spared discomfort. Sparing the child from uncomfortable experiences is not always a good idea. Aside from this, and an even greater disadvantage of not telling the truth, is the lack of trust in his parents that will occur when the child learns, as he so often does, that his parents lied to him.

Parents who are involved in some of the situations discussed in this book may have their own particular problems. After all, they too are affected emotionally and have doubts and misgivings. This makes it harder for them to offer the type of stability and support that their children require in times of extraordinary stress. Some parents may be disturbed to the point that therapy is necessary before they can adequately cope with their children in periods of crisis. But even parents who are not so seriously disturbed may be at a loss to know what is the best way to handle a situation. Given some guidelines, they could offer greater support and understanding to their children.

This book hopes to aid parents and surrogate parents in thinking about, knowing about, and having a better understanding of what we might tell children, both in our words and our behavior, especially at times of stress or when significant events are taking place in their lives. No one can tell parents exactly what words to use in every situation that arises, but we can combine some knowledge and common sense and then do the best we can.

All of us who are parents find ourselves somewhat in the same boat. A person trained to work with parents and children may have an advantage: he has seen and learned from a large number of different types of families. The ideas presented here have developed from impressions gained and advice given in twenty years of practice, first as a pediatrician, subsequently as a psychiatrist, and throughout as a parent.

CHAPTER I

The Family

Parents and the Blame for Children's Problems

"Tell me," said one of the doctor's old acquaintances, "now that you've been in child psychiatry for a while, is it true that when kids have emotional problems, it's always the parents' fault?"

THIS IS a question I have been asked on innumerable occasions; undoubtedly, other physicians have heard it too.

Parents are often blamed for all the problems of their children. Even when not reproached by others, some parents needlessly punish themselves by assuming that everything that has gone wrong in the life of their child is their fault. At the opposite pole we find individuals who feel that nothing that happens in the life of their offspring is a reflection on the parents. It is always "the school's fault" or because of "the neighborhood children" or "the effects of television."

It is true that parents are a most important influence in the lives of their children, but there are no perfect parents. In no way can anyone give us instructions for being infallible parents, and in reality there is no need for perfection. Even when intellectually we might know "the right thing to do," our emotions intervene and we do not always stop and think, "Are we doing the right thing?"

In fact, if "the perfect parent" existed, it would be most difficult for the child who had to be brought up by him. Imagine how the youngster with all his gropings and stumblings would feel were he brought up by a parent who never made a mistake, who always did the right thing. In such a situation the child would feel excessively guilty about any anger he might have toward his perfect parent. He would be afraid of making a mistake, and his feelings of inadequacy would be greatly exaggerated if he was always comparing himself to a parent who was never wrong. Fortunately, since we are all human and imperfect, no child will be exposed to our hypothetical paragon.

Still, there are parents who act as if they were perfect. This type of parent can never admit to his child, or even to himself, that he has made a mistake, especially when it relates to what he expects of the youngster. In contrast, another type of parent apologizes all too frequently. This parent is insecure in his concepts of child rearing; he feels that he is being a poor parent most of the time. And by his constant waverings and subsequent apologies, he communicates these insecurities to his children.

We do not have to do the "right thing" 100 percent of the time in order for things to go well in the parent-child relationship. As parents we can allow ourselves a margin for error. But there is a vast difference between acting in a beneficial manner 85 percent of the time or only 15 percent of the time. There is a tremendous drive toward normality in most youngsters; they can tolerate some inadequacies but not if these are extreme.

It is well to remember that many factors influence our reactions to our children and their responses to us. No two human beings are exactly alike. This is of special note when dealing with siblings. People sometimes make comparisons between family members saying, "How can two children be so different when they come from the same family and have grown up in the same environment?" Such a question obviously proceeds from an erroneous assumption.

As a matter of fact, no two siblings grow up in identical circumstances. Perhaps the closest approximation to such a setting would be the situation of healthy identical twins in a family where there are no other children. Nevertheless, when considering emotions and interpersonal relationships, the family that has a second baby is no longer providing the same environment that existed when there was only one child. Additionally, the economic conditions of the family may change greatly from the time of their first child until the birth of their second, third, or fourth baby. So, in the broadest sense, each child in a family does not grow up in the same environment.

Every baby has a different makeup or constitution. Some infants are more active from the time they are born, while others are more passive. In the nursery of a maternity ward one newborn may be wriggling around and crying lustily when he is hungry or uncomfortable. Another may be considerably quieter in his reaction to discomfort. As each infant grows and develops, his particular makeup affects the interaction between him and his parents. Some of us can be fairly comfortable with the job of raising a passive baby, but not nearly so comfortable with an extremely active one.

There are certain infants who from the beginning are hypersensitive in special ways. For example, a particular baby's skin may be so sensitive that he will cry merely on being touched, and his mother may not be able to hold him and cuddle him. The mother may wonder why the baby reacts to her in this way and, depending on her background, she may entertain the thought that she is a "rejecting mother." Yet, if this same infant were first placed on a pillow that would act as a shield to his sensitive skin, and then held by the parent, the crying would probably cease. Another infant may react uncomfortably to sound, and this too will influence how he is affected by his surroundings.

Besides these constitutional differences in newborns, some infants suffer mild brain damage during their development in the uterus, or as a consequence of the birth process. The effects of this minimal nervous system abnormality may not be readily apparent, but the reactions of such a child may be different from a child who does not have this condition. Children who are affected in this manner can compensate for their difficulties as they grow and develop, but problems can arise with such children that are not the fault of the parents.

We, as parents, also learn in the process of raising our offspring. Many of us, prior to the arrival of our babies, have preconceived notions of what kind of parents we will be and how we will raise our children. We find, especially with our first child, that our ideas do not always work, and we have to change some of these methods.

The people who are most often dogmatically authoritative about the rearing of children are those who have not had any children and have not had to test out their ideas. They quickly tell you that all your child needs is a little discipline, and if he were their child he would not be acting this way. A friend, who is a pediatrician and had practiced for several years before he married and became a father, said that he was quite shaken and insecure after his first son was born. He became aware that the advice he was now giving parents differed markedly from what he had formerly given. Before long he recovered from his turmoil and felt that he was a better doctor and more sensitive to the problems of the parents as well as the children.

When we say that parents are not to blame for all their children's problems we should keep in mind that, besides the factors already mentioned, youngsters in their development are affected by the subculture they live in, the socioeconomic conditions of their family, the neighborhood, educational experiences, illnesses, and relationships with peers and significant adults with whom they come in contact. Parents, of course, have a great responsibility. They are the primary protectors of the child and the interpretors to him of many aspects of his environment. What follows here is designed to help parents in carrying out these important functions.

The Job of a Father

In the theater lobby Mrs. Keith approached a physician and said, "I must tell you this. I was riding down Nevada Avenue with a friend of mine and, when we passed your house, there you were and you were holding onto your son and shaking him. I turned to my friend and said, 'There's a pediatric psychiatrist.'"

"That's a good story," said the doctor, "but it's not true."

"What do you mean?" retorted the lady indignantly. "I saw you. You were shaking him."

"That's right. You saw me and I was shaking him because he was running out into the street. But I wasn't a pediatric psychiatrist. I was his father and I was shaking him."

No MATTER what other vocation we may have, each of us who has children has a most important job to do: being a parent. We tell our offspring a lot by the manner in which we fulfill this role.

I have always wanted to write an article entitled "Balancing the Seesaw." It has occurred to me that, in our culture, fathers cope with two conflicting priorities. The years during which a man is engaged in building up his reputation in a business or profession are the very years that his children require his presence most. By the time a father has made his mark in the world, his offspring are usually in their teens and becoming more involved with their peer group. At this point they should not need him as much as before.

Every father has to struggle with this balancing act. Too frequently the job of being a father is the one that is neglected. Many men give the welfare of their families as their reason for working so hard. Then, because work has been so tiring, they spend the evening unwinding and reading the newspaper, and the weekends playing golf. Their youngsters rarely have the opportunity to spend much time with Father.

At times we wonder why these men even had children, for they don't appear to enjoy a relationship with them. There are too many "fatherless" boys and girls around. It is amazing to see teen-agers who are unable to provide an adequate answer when asked what kind of work their father actually does.

Children are a mixed blessing. A good bit of the time they are a pain in the neck, especially the younger ones. Their presence as members of our family deprives us of some of our freedom. But they can also be a great source of pleasure. If we cannot accept both parts of this proposition, we would be more honest and perhaps better off if we did not have children.

One father stated that, in trying to make more and more money, his purpose was to leave a proper financial legacy for his son, just as his parent had done for him. He gave this explanation when asked why he did not spend more time with his boy, who at that juncture was having problems. This father already had sufficient means to take very good care of his family. The greatest gift he could have given his son was to help him develop a healthy personality and self-esteem. With these assets the young man could make his own way in the world, even if his father lost all his money.

Fathers need to be available if they are going to help their offspring learn about life. There are times when a psychiatrist sees a child who says little and seems to do little during his therapy hours, and yet he improves. When we wonder why this improvement occurs, we realize that the young patient has had at least fifty minutes of undivided attention from the doctor. How many of us devote an equal period each week of complete attentiveness to each individual child in our family? When a parent spends some time simply being with his child, he is often startled to hear the things that concern his youngster and the questions he asks. No doubt all children have things on their mind that they want to talk about, but they won't do so if they feel that Father isn't interested.

In former years of less complicated technology, smaller businesses, and more rural environments, many of us worked side by side with our fathers. Occasionally we may have resented this, but we did get to spend considerable time with our fathers and to know a good deal about them. We found things in them that we liked and others that we did not care for. We might have decided that in some ways we wanted to be like our fathers, but in other areas we would want to act differently. But we knew what Father was like, and chances are he knew a lot about us too.

In these days circumstances are usually such that most boys are not automatically thrown together with their fathers. So often Father works in the city and the family lives in the suburbs. It is, therefore, critical for us to make a conscientious effort to provide sufficient contact between ourselves and our children.

Especially during their formative years we must balance the demands of our business or occupation with the needs of our youngsters. No one can dictate exactly how and in what proportions we should do this. But it is crystal clear to anyone who works with upset children, or who cares about the problems of young people, that the lack of a father is a prime cause of difficulties in many boys and girls. A parent can forsake his family in two ways: he may actually leave them or he may desert them in an emotional sense by his utter preoccupation with his own work and recreation.

Being with one's child does not mean doing everything for him. Some fathers become so impatient that they don't permit a youngster to learn from his own mistakes. Most of us know that if our son helps us with a job around the house it usually takes about twice as long than if we did it alone. But the child benefits from working at the task together with us.

We have to tell our children that they should expose themselves to new experiences even though it makes them anxious. We should not always attempt to make things easy for them if they encounter a problem that is upsetting to them. The overcoming of anxiety enables them to grow and develop, and eventually to be on their own.

Children should be permitted to make decisions that affect them, providing that the matters to be decided do not carry with them the prospect of severe physical injury or other drastic consequences. Parents should look at the pros and cons of a particular situation facing the child, and determine whether or not the decision can be left to the youngsters. Even if the results of their choices are emotionally painful to them, we can let them learn in this manner. But we have to be around to lend them support.

A junior high school student was much upset because he had a biology teacher who was very demanding and hard on the class. This sensitive youngster came home from school each evening terribly agitated. He was afraid that he was going to fail the course. His parents felt that perhaps it wasn't worth it to go through this agony every night, and they were tempted to remove him from the class. Nevertheless, they did not. Instead, the father spent a considerable amount of time talking with his son, and trying to determine why he was so upset. He made suggestions to him as to how he might handle his notes and encouraged him to do the best he could, emphasizing that the grade he got was not of paramount importance. The young man settled down and began to improve in his work. By the end of the year he not only received an *A* in biology, but he also developed a real interest in the subject.

It would have been much easier for the father to simply get his son out of that particular teacher's class, but had he done so, the boy would not have had the benefit of overcoming what seemed like an insurmountable obstacle. This triumph would have a salutary effect on the boy's personality development, but to accomplish it required the presence and support of his father.

Our sons' ideas of how to be a father should come from us. In order to let a boy know what a good father is supposed to do, we must be around enough of the time to show him. We often hear the statement that we have "to cut the umbilical cord." If we make ourselves available to a child, and meet his needs, he will reach the point where he no longer needs us, and he will grow up with a built-in awareness of what a good father does. The umbilical cord need not be cut abruptly. At the proper time it should simply have withered away.

The Job of a Mother

In the last act of a show put on by a medical fraternity about fifteen years ago, the time that the action was supposed to take place was "the future." The roles of men and women had become reversed. The wives were going to medical school and there was one "token male" in the class. The husbands stayed at home and cared for the children. They were also members of a "Medical Students' Husbands Association" and in the show they sang a song about their not enjoying the cleaning, cooking, shopping, and caring for the kids. Their song included the following lines:

> *The girls still make an awful fuss*
> *Because we have no uterus.*

NATURE HAS dictated that at least one function of women cannot be taken over by the men. Fifteen years ago this was a joke, but today many women are rebelling against what previously were considered traditional feminine roles.

For a long time, girls in our culture have been faced with a problem. They are sent to school, encouraged to go to college, and perhaps trained for a profession. Then they marry, have children, and find themselves tied down to work that is drudgery for them. Along with this, as they were growing up they did not develop a feeling that being a mother is really a worthwhile endeavor.

Their husbands often forget that their wives ever had other aspirations. The man may also feel it is unmanly for him to change a diaper, warm a formula bottle, or help with any household chore. His wife may become bored and angry, and consequently have little patience with their offspring.

As much as children need a father around when they are growing up, the need for a mother is of even greater importance particularly during infancy and preschool years. While mothers may or may not breast-feed their babies, the cuddling, closeness, and tactile stimulation that should go with feeding are all very important for the healthy emotional, as well as physical, development of the human being.

A few years ago an eight-month-old infant, admitted to the hospital because of a physical condition, seemed to be retarded. He did not smile and was slow in his physical development. We learned that he had not received much attention from his mother.

We assigned one nurse to take care of this boy; she was responsible for feeding him, changing him, and dressing him. We also encouraged her to spend extra time with him, holding him, talking to him, and just playing with him. It was remarkable and wonderful to see this baby change. He began to smile. He was more alert and began to develop so rapidly that the staff no longer considered him retarded.

In another instance, a three-month-old girl, who had weighed six pounds ten ounces at birth, was admitted to the hospital weighing seven pounds six ounces. She had gained very little from the time of her birth and was an irritable, poorly developed, and emaciated-looking baby. She vomited varying amounts of food after her feedings. All the tests done by the physicians showed no abnormalities.

Doctors observed that she sucked her fingers and used her tongue in a way to make herself vomit, so restraints were applied to her arms. But this did no good. She was then seen by the psychiatrist, and a program was instituted to provide more satisfaction for the infant. The restraints were removed. A special nurse who acted as a substitute mother was assigned to care for this patient. Various ways of entertaining her, especially after feedings, were utilized, such as rolling her in a carriage and holding her for certain periods. She responded to these measures by a progressive lessening of the vomiting, and she gained weight. After three weeks of this treatment, she had gained over two pounds.

These are but two examples out of many that could demonstrate the infant's need for a single mothering figure to take care of him.

There should be no argument about women receiving equal pay for equal work. Nor should there be any disagreement about equality of opportunity for women when it comes to a career. Yet, if a woman wants children and chooses to have them, she should at least be with them and care for them especially until they are of school age. After that, she should try to be in the home by the time the children return from school.

It has often been said that a good maid is better than a bad mother. However true this may be, there is no adequate substitute for a good mother. If a mother must go to work because of financial necessity, she should try to provide the best substitute possible to care for her children.

Fathers should realize that while their work may be difficult, it is a diversion for them that their wives do not have. One woman, whom I know well, has recommended that each father be required to spend one whole week a year at home so that he will really know what his wife experiences. Fathers should understand that it is essential for their children's welfare to have a mother at home, and they should do whatever they can to relieve her of some of the drudgery in the evenings and on weekends. There is no reason why husbands should not help with diapers and occasional feedings.

If fathers have an understanding and helpful attitude toward their wives, women may feel better about caring for their children and enjoy them more. In this way, our children may grow up with the conviction that being a mother serves a significant and useful purpose. Just as Father, by his behavior, tells his son that being a father is worthwhile, so does Mother's way of mothering instruct her daughter.

Affluence

"Damn it," said an annoyed Mr. Shelly to his son. "You don't appreciate anything. Here you have your own air-conditioned room, a radio, a TV, a tape recorder, and an electric typewriter. Why, when I was your age I shared a hallway with my brother."

"That's right," said the teen-age son, "but compared to your father, you probably had it better than I do compared to you."

How MANY of us have said, or felt like saying, the words spoken by this father to his son. Today we are constantly asserting, or being told by others, that affluence is the cause of drug problems, of student unrest, and of various ills of the younger generation.

We tend to forget that while middle-class youngsters have more in the way of material possessions than their parents did, those same parents in many instances had much more than the grandparents. It was true that Mr. Shelly and his brother had shared a studio couch in a hallway, but their father had a much more difficult childhood. He had gone away from home at the age of ten to work in another village. When he was living at home, he shared one room with six other members of his family. As a fifteen-year-old, he immigrated to the United States where for his first two weeks' work he received two dollars, fifty cents of which he sent to his parents in Poland.

Compared to his own father, Mr. Shelly had lived a life of relative comfort. He never went hungry during the depression years. He may not have enjoyed many luxuries, but he was taken care of adequately. He attended college and graduate school, most of which was paid for by his father.

We can see that Mr. Shelly was obviously annoyed when he made the statement about the boy's lack of appreciation, but he would not say today that the comfortable life had affected his son adversely. The young man is now a junior in college. He does not take drugs. He does not burn down college buildings or destroy property. He dislikes injustice. He stands up for his rights and the rights of others. He is taking advantage of opportunities to learn, and although not concerned primarily with getting good grades he is getting them anyway. It is true that he will not work solely for the sake of making money, but he is ready to work if he is learning something, and would be willing to work at any job if his parents told him it was a financial necessity.

Affluence is not the cause of the many problems that are so readily attributed to it. If parents give money and expensive objects to children as substitutes for time and attention, the youngsters' difficulties are not the result of living too comfortable a life. Our youth may be suffering from what we have not given of ourselves rather than from what we have given of our means. All things being equal, abject poverty will have a much more adverse effect on personality development and ambition than will the affluent situation. It's neither especially healthy, or enjoyable, to be poor. Ask the man who's been there.

In the handling of our material resources, the example we set for our children is of great consequence. We communicate a lot to children by our reasons for doing what we do. A child will have one view if he knows that his father purchased a Cadillac because it was a car he could afford, would enjoy driving, and felt it had mechanical advantages over other automobiles. The youngster will have quite another outlook if he knows that his parent bought a Cadillac because it was the "thing to do" in his neighborhood, and Dad did not want to be different.

Money has so many varied meanings to people. Wealthy children have told me that they wished to be poor because they felt they would be happier poor and would have fewer problems. Poor children feel they would not have problems at all if only they had money. Certainly the latter may be closer to the truth, but neither group would find that a state of being richer or poorer would bring a solution to all their difficulties.

Material possessions make life comfortable and more enjoyable; they do not, in and of themselves, destroy initiative in a child. A youngster may ask for and receive something not because he needs it for a particular purpose, but rather because most of the children in the neighborhood have it. A parent may go along with such a request solely because he doesn't want his child to be unhappy. This is a mistake. He is essentially giving the child a message which says that self-esteem does not depend on what is within oneself, but on one's possessions.

In other words, it is not what or how much we give our youngsters that is of importance, but the reasons we have for giving and what they learn from us about the use and meaning of money and possessions.

The Family: An Emotional Laboratory

Stuart came down to breakfast angry with his brother for some reason.

"I hate you, Andrew," he said. "I wish you'd go kill yourself."

"You'd like that, wouldn't you?" replied his brother.

WHEN MOST of us were young, our parents, on hearing an exchange such as this, might have cried out, "What a terrible thing to say to your brother!" Perhaps many parents would still say this today. Had we observed these two boys an hour later, however, we would have seen them walking down the street with their arms around each other's shoulders.

The family setting should be a sort of unself-conscious laboratory for learning and experimentation, especially so in relation to how one handles his feelings. None of us would expect a teen-ager to finish junior high school and then, without further training, go out into the community and function as an engineer, plumber, physician, lawyer, electrician, or in any other occupation requiring knowledge and skill. Yet, we sometimes expect our children to act grown-up without experiencing a period of trial and error in the use and control of their emotions.

Were we to listen to a tape recording of only the angry exchanges occurring between some parents and their offspring, we might assume that they have a horrible relationship. But very often this conclusion would be wrong. For the same parents and children who have the freedom to be furious with each other can have the greatest mutual respect. And most of the time they are not angry. If parents and their youngsters exist in a state of habitual exasperation with each other, something is definitely amiss. On the other hand, if they are never provoked with one another, something is wrong also.

There is no way to prevent feelings of frustration in the human infant. If he is hungry or uncomfortable his needs should be met, but we cannot satisfy him instantly. There will be a lag between the time he experiences his discomfort and the moment that the breast or bottle is given to him. When a child is frustrated he becomes angry. Ideally, each person must find acceptable and relatively comfortable ways to handle anger.

Too many children begin to feel unreasonably guilty about their hostile feelings. Assume that a child throws a toy at his mother when he is angry. Usually he is told, "You're not to throw things at your mother." This is true. Nevertheless, the youngster may also get the impression from such a statement that he is not supposed to feel anger toward his parent. This creates difficulties for him because he cannot help feeling resentful. We should aid the child by giving him permission for the anger but not for his actions. We can tell him it is all right to feel as if he wants to throw a toy at his mother, but that it should not be thrown because it might hurt her or do other damage. If every one of us who ever felt like shooting someone was put in jail, we would all be there together. Laws should not punish us for our thoughts or feelings but only for our acts.

Youngsters need to learn that they may have feelings, but they must be responsible for their actions. When a child calls a parent "stupid," we would be well advised to translate this into "I'm angry" and not get into a battle over the word. When the relationship between the parent and child is basically good, he will not grow up believing he has a stupid parent.

Siblings, like the boys quoted above, have periodic hostility toward each other. Here too, as with parent and child, we should become concerned if they exhibit nothing but angry feeling or if they never show angry feeling at all. A parent who has been an only child often finds it extremely difficult to understand and tolerate the periodic bickering that goes on between his children. He has not lived through this experience himself. Such a parent, seeing his own youngsters arguing and fighting, may think, "If I had had brothers and sisters I wouldn't have acted that way." It is important for him to understand that, within limits, the disagreements and displays of irritation by his children toward each other are normal.

When children who have been very inhibited in expressing their anger toward their parents have a period of therapy, they may begin to express anger more directly. So often it is striking to note that, coincident with the parents' report that the child expresses hostility more openly, they also relate that their offspring is more affectionate and in general showing greater evidence of love. It is as if the youngster who has to put a damper on his feelings of anger also must cover up other sentiments, including love.

We want our children to act responsibly, but we should not want them to carry around a burden of unwarranted guilt simply because they feel angry at times.

Authority

Ralph, told that he was not to go out after dinner, became very angry with his father.

"You can't tell me what to do," he argued. "The Constitution guarantees me the right of life, liberty, and the pursuit of happiness."

CHANCES ARE that many of us have heard this type of legalistic argument from our children when they are confronted with the limitations we must periodically put on their behavior. The implication of Ralph's statement is that the family is a democracy and parents have no right to tell their child what to do.

A family is not a democratic body to be ruled by a consensus. Parents should be in charge. Children are not born with built-in controls. These need to be developed. Their elders must be prepared to exercise their prerogatives as heads of the household. In discharging this function, however, they should not expect their decisions always to be met with good-natured acceptance on the part of their offspring.

Parents must be willing to say "No," whether this be to the four-year-old who wants another toy each time he enters a store, to the ten-year-old who wants to see one more television show before he goes to bed, or to the adolescent who wants to change all the rules. Too many mothers and fathers are so concerned with having their children like them all the time that they essentially abdicate their parental role. To be good parents we must be willing to be temporarily unpopular in the eyes of our children. When we tell a youngster to do something he doesn't want to do, there is no reason why he must accept our demand with utter joy. But his unhappiness must not keep us from doing our duty as we see it. We should be prepared for his angry reaction and not let such an outburst dissuade us.

How do we reply to a boy who confronts us in lawyer-like fashion with the Constitution? We can tell him that the provisions of this historic document do not apply in our home. As far as his life in our country is concerned, we would hope that each citizen would be granted these rights, even though this does not always seem to be the case. Where family life is involved, however, we certainly have a right to establish reasonable standards and to expect them to be followed.

We can inform the young man that we have to support him, and in a large measure we might be held legally responsible for any flagrant misbehavior on his part. Therefore, as long as he is living in our household, he will be responsible for following our guidelines. At the point where he feels able to leave and support himself adequately with no help from us, he will no longer be subject to our direction and control. We will be willing to listen to any objections he has to our rules and we will take his criticism into account, but if we still feel we have made a correct decision he will be expected to conform to our requests.

Parental Consistency

"Mrs. Walter," asked the physician, "why do you give in to your children all the time?"

"But I have to, Doctor," was the reply. "My husband is so strict with them I have to make up for it."

Mrs. Walter's approach is encountered often. In the rearing of their children, a father may be operating at one pole while the mother functions at the opposite one. Each maintains that his (or her) action is necessary to counterbalance the spouse's way of doing things.

When people ask me to state in as few words as possible how children should be treated, my answer is "With kindness, firmness, and consistency." Kindness should not equal complete permissiveness. Firmness does not mean punishment. Consistency need not indicate rigidity. None of the three excludes the others. If we apply these principles in most of our dealings with our offspring, we and they will benefit.

Some children become experts at playing one parent against the other. They quickly exploit existing differences between their mother and father. A child may be refused permission for an action or object by his mother and then go to the father with the same demand, never mentioning the fact that he has already been turned down. The parent who has said "No" can become very angry, believing that her refusal has been consciously countermanded by her husband.

Youngsters need to be handled as consistently as possible. In rearing our children none of us acts in a constant way 100 percent of the time. Nevertheless, in our individual dealings with them, each of us should be as consistent as is feasible. In addition, a father and mother should attempt to achieve a united front in the management of their children.

A parent makes a dreadful mistake if he believes that by behaving in an opposite fashion he can compensate for undesirable actions of his mate. Rather than do this he should say what he thinks is being done incorrectly. Such discussion should be conducted out of earshot of the children. Parents who have markedly different ideas concerning the handling of their youngsters should make every effort to compromise and decide on a common method of dealing with them.

If both parents are at home and a child comes to one of them with a request, he should be asked if he has already spoken to the other. Frequently the reply will be "Yes," and if so, the child should be told that what the first parent said goes. He should be reminded that if Mother says "No" he need not come to Father with the same demand.

It is often tempting to a parent, because of anger toward one's spouse, to give in to a youngster's plea for something already turned down by the other parent. We should remember that such behavior harms the child much more than it does the mother or father involved. When a child manipulates a situation so that he gets his way from one after being refused by the other, he should be told that his action was unacceptable and that such maneuvers should not be attempted in the future.

No matter whether we are strict or liberal with our children, by being consistent we tell them we mean what we say. They, in turn, can be more sure of where they stand and will be more comfortable because of this.

Physical Punishment

The hard-hit baseball shattered the windshield of a neighbor's automobile. Mike, the fourteen-year-old who had batted the ball, walked up to the neighbor's door, rang the bell, informed the car's owner of the occurrence, and told him he would pay for the damage.

"Thank you," said the neighbor, "I wouldn't have known who did it."

Later, when he spoke to the boy's father, the neighbor said, "You must not have spared the belt on your son for him to behave so well."

UNFORTUNATELY, THE idea is prevalent in some quarters that a child must have received spankings or whippings if he behaves himself well and acts as a responsible human being.

Mike, who broke the window and immediately made it known, had never been spanked in his life.

Too often in recent days we hear that we will spoil the child if we spare the rod. Articles appear in the press atributing drug abuse, college protest, and all real or imagined transgressions of the younger generation to permissiveness—a term never really defined. The implication is that if we are tough enough on children they will grow up to be law-abiding citizens, but if we are not rough with them all will be lost.

Do we really spoil youngsters if we spare the rod? Do children have to be spanked? Are we depriving them of proper discipline if they are not beaten for each misdeed or every time they "talk back" to their parents?

It is a fact that there are children who are spanked occasionally and who still get along well with their parents. This depends on the meaning of the punishment to both parents and offspring, and on the existence of other positive elements in the family's relationships. Such children can grow up to be perfectly decent individuals.

Nevertheless, it is also true that there are as many youngsters who are never spanked and whose actions and values are beyond reasonable reproach. They too mature and become fine adults.

Physical punishment is not a required ingredient for the development of a satisfactory moral sense and acceptable behavior. Children can be conditioned to have a fear of beatings and may control some of their acts because of this. Still, we cannot make them afraid of everything, and a conscience based on the fear of being beaten will be a conscience with a large number of holes in it.

Let us not assume from the foregoing that children do not need discipline. A good parent is one who tells his offspring what the limits are and then sees to it that they adhere to these guidelines, even though the children may complain bitterly. Ultimately the most adequate type of control will be the self-discipline that the young person develops within himself. Some form of punishment is necessary at times when family rules are broken by a child, but the punishment need not be the application of the father's fist, strap, or hairbrush. Let me also add that most parents on occasion swat a child in a moment of anger, but this is quite different than the use of frequent thrashings.

What do we tell a youngster when we freely employ physical punishment? We let him know by our action that we disapprove of his behavior, but there are other ways of delivering this message. By excessive spanking, however, we also tell him that physical violence is to be used to control people. We are also exposing him to a double standard; namely, it is permissible for us to hit him, yet he is forbidden to strike us. Some people will argue, "But, because parents do something it doesn't mean their children can do the same thing." This certainly should be true in many activities, but if we beat a child we will find ourselves on shaky ground when we try to tell him he must not do the same to his siblings, parents, or playmates.

Besides these general considerations for the avoidance of hitting as a punitive measure, there is another reason related to a child's stage of development and normal fears. Young children, between the ages of eighteen months and four years, are normally afraid of harm occurring to a part of their body. When we strike a child who is struggling with this fear, we will only be adding to his concern. Even the parent who believes strongly in spanking should be mindful of the fears that may exist in his youngster.

There are other types of punishment that we can employ. Children can be deprived of certain privileges. The use of favored objects can be prohibited for a period of time. For very young children, simply stopping them from continuing the activity we disapprove of and making them sit quietly next to us for a while may be an effective method. A child can be sent to his room. The list of alternatives can go on and on. Each parent, if he looks about him, can determine what will apply best in his household. We should not do things that aggravate existing fears, for example, locking a child in a closet or other small confined space. We should also avoid constantly threatening punishments and then being inconsistent about applying them. In the long run our hope is that the youngster will discipline himself because he wants to, and this desire will be based on what kind of relationship he has with his parents.

An occasional strong tap on the backside may clear the air for both parent and child, but repeated strappings for the purpose of teaching a lesson may teach the child all the wrong lessons about the use of force.

Moral Teaching

Brian handed his dad seventy-two cents.
"What's this for?" asked his father.
"It belongs to you."
"Where did it come from?"
"I sold my sheet music of 'Snoopy and the Red Baron' to my friend next door, but I hadn't bought it with my allowance. You bought it for me so the money belongs to you."

BRIAN, LIKE most boys his age, enjoyed accumulating cash, but he gave the money to his father. Only he knew of the sale and the payment he received. He acted as he did because it was the right thing to do, not because he was afraid he would be punished for keeping the money.

His father respected and appreciated the boy's behavior and accepted the money rather than tell him he could keep it for himself. The youngster's act, while relatively unimportant as an isolated incident, indicated that he had learned his lessons well; namely, that he always should try to do what he considered to be right simply because it was right, and not because he might be punished if caught doing something wrong.

This boy was not born knowing how to behave in situations like this one. His conduct reflects the type of moral teaching that had been attempted, by word and example, throughout his life. For instance, when eating in one of the restaurants of a large chain, he asked his father why the waitress was told when she undercharged them, for the company would not miss the money. The boy was told that this was the honest thing to do, and he was reminded that on occasions when the check showed an overcharge, the waitress had also been told.

Children learn through these experiences. It is important for us as parents to give our offspring good moral teaching. Hopefully, we will have a decent outlook on what is right and what is wrong and we will transmit these values to our children.

Few of us agree completely on what we consider right, but too often people seem to operate on the principle of "anything goes as long as you don't get caught." Too seldom do we stop to consider if our actions are infringing on the rights and welfare of others. When we have done something wrong we may not even be honest with ourselves to the extent of feeling legitimate guilt for our actions, but rather we seek rationalizations to prove our behavior was proper.

It has been my impression in practicing child psychiatry that there seems to be a correlation between the troubles of some young patients and the manner in which their parents pay their bills. For example, one college-age young man had very little genuine self-esteem. He drove a Thunderbird, went to Florida during the winter school vacation, and planned to spend his summer touring Europe. He recounted how his father always underbid on government contracts knowing he would more than make up for this with overcharges on changes made in the course of the job. The boy regarded cheating on one's income tax as usual and acceptable procedure. While his father lavished cars and trips on his son, he only paid his medical bills after being threatened with a lawsuit. So often, children who have not been taught to have regard for their obligations and for the rights of others end up with an inadequate identity of their own.

Another father told his son that he should not behave in a certain manner because it would bring discredit on the family name, and he reminded him that his grandfather had been an important man in the community. We should tell our children that they should do the proper thing because it is right, rather than because it will affect their (and our) good name.

Several years ago a group of boys in a suburban community was apprehended by the police for stealing cars and joyriding. The parents were upset to find their upper-middle-class youngsters breaking the law. Few of them connected their children's offenses with the fact that the parents had demonstrated lack of respect for law by permitting their offspring to learn how to drive before they were old enough to obtain a learner's permit legally. When a fifteen-year-old asks us to let him drive the car on his home street, we should tell him, "It is against the law for you to drive until you are the legal age, and we will not allow you to do so."

Recently some fairly well-to-do boys committed acts of vandalism in their neighborhood. Their parents were informed by a neighbor of what had occurred. The attitude of some of the parents was, "Don't bother me. I've reported it to my insurance company and they'll take care of the damage." With parental attitudes like these, can we blame the children for the delinquent behavior? The youngster should be told, "You have done something wrong and you will have to pay for it. You will either get a job and make some money or we will give you things to do to earn enough to pay for the damage you've done. You also must go and apologize."

When a parent's insurance policy is paying for the damage, the child should earn money to pay part of the insurance premiums.

We should tell our children that we expect them to be aware of what is right and what is wrong and to act accordingly. We should tell them that they must consider whether their own actions result in unfairness to another person. They should be taught to regard others as fellow beings rather than as objects to be exploited. In all these matters we will tell them much more by our example than by our words. A child will not believe honesty is a virtue if he sees his father cheating in business.

I have seen children beaten for lying and being told, "Lying is one thing we won't tolerate around here." The same youngsters overhear their mother refuse someone's request over the phone, saying, "I'm sorry I can't do it, I've a terrible headache" or, "I'm going out of town tomorrow." Neither statement is in any way the truth.

None of us are truthful and honest 100 percent of the time. But at least let us try to be aware of what we are doing and saying, and how these actions compare with what we are telling our children.

One young man told his father, "You should realize something. The way you've taught us to do the right thing, even though it isn't easy or convenient, is not the way most people live today." Unfortunately, his parent had to agree with this statement, but told him this was an even stronger reason for trying to live in a moral way.

CHAPTER II

Doctors, Hospitals, and Operations

Introduction

How would you like to be taken from your house to a strange place where people you did not know would hurt you? The thought alone is frightening, but essentially that is what often happens to many of our children. To a youngster who has not been prepared beforehand, the trip to a hospital for an operation constitutes a strange and frightening experience.

Even periodic visits to the physician for a routine physical examination can produce uncomfortable ideas and feelings in the child's mind. He may be wondering why certain things are done to him and be afraid to ask. Often the things that bother children are either not apparent to adults or simply overlooked. Too frequently, competent physicians neglect the significant area of giving both child and adult patients an adequate explanation, in uncomplicated terms, of what will be happening to the patient.

Let us assume that your physician informs you that your son or daughter needs an operation. It is likely that your child has never had to be hospitalized before, and it is likely that this will not be the only hospitalization of his lifetime. Therefore, it is of extreme importance that the child be prepared for this event so that he makes the best adjustment possible to it and to any future hospitalization.

A child who knows what is going to happen may still have fear, but the fear will be much greater if he is led, or tricked, into a totally unfamiliar situation. It is important to be truthful with your child. His questions should be answered to the best of your ability. On the whole, when given truthful information youngsters react adequately.

Parents often do not possess the knowledge necessary to answer the child's questions about hospitalization and operations. This section discusses some of the factual information about the more common operations of childhood: tonsillectomy, hernia repair, and fractures and their healing.

Do not hesitate to ask your own physician for any other information or explanation that you may need in order to furnish sufficient support to your child. Some parents are reluctant to bother the doctor, but helping the child with his fear is of greater importance than the possibility of hurting the doctor's feelings. If, for any reason, you cannot explain things to your child, ask the physician to do so, and request that he do it in language that the child will understand.

Visits to the Doctor

The little boy returned from his visit to the doctor for a routine physical checkup. "I was scared," he said. "Why did they take out so much of my blood?"

THERE ARE some things about a routine visit to the doctor that may be frightening to a child. We should do whatever we can to prevent unnecessary fears and misconceptions.

At the doctor's office, the young patient is usually weighed and measured. He is examined by the physician who uses various instruments: a stethoscope with which he listens to the sounds of the heart and lungs; an otoscope with which he can look into the ears, nose, mouth, and throat; a sphygmomanometer for checking the blood pressure; and an ophthalmoscope for examining the eyes. The doctor also feels the abdomen and other parts of the child's body. Not every physician does all these things at each examination.

In addition to the physical examination, the child may have a blood count or other type of blood test. A urine specimen may also be requested. At periodic intervals the child will be given immunization injections, commonly referred to as "booster shots." And on some occasions X-rays of his lungs or bones may be part of the examination procedure.

Occasionally, the child may be referred to a roentgoenologist (X-ray specialist) for more specialized examinations; for example, gastrointestinal studies where the child will be examined in a darkened room by a fluoroscope and be asked to drink a chalky suspension of barium; or urinary tract X-rays where a dye will be injected into a vein before the pictures are taken.

There may be other less common specialized types of tests recommended or performed by the physician. The electroencephalogram (brain wave test) is not an unusual procedure and one which children might easily fear and misinterpret.

Youngsters can have concerns about some of the ordinary aspects of the periodic health examination to which their parents and physicians may not be attentive. Imagine a six-year-old at the doctors' office for an examination. At some point, either the physician or one of his assistants will stick the child's finger (which hurts) and then will proceed to suck his blood out through a little glass tube, seemingly to the doctor's mouth. The wide-eyed child, who may have seen vampires on television, is greatly concerned that he may be harmed by losing this blood which is being taken from him. In reality the amount of blood he loses is about 0.1 cc, a very tiny amount compared to the total quantity of blood in a person's body. But the child does not know this and conceivably can be frightened unnecessarily.

With about fifteen seconds of explanation to the young patient, much good can be accomplished. Before he has his finger stuck, the youngster can be told either by the parent or the doctor, "Johnny, the doctor is going to stick your finger and it hurts a little. You might even feel like sticking him back. He's going to take a tiny bit of blood out. This won't make you different in any way, and checking on the blood helps him make sure that everything is O.K. with you."

Such an explanation accomplishes several purposes. First, it establishes trust on the part of the child; you are being honest with him when you tell him that "it hurts a little." Second, it gives the child permission for angry feelings, which he certainly may have if someone hurts him, by telling him "you might feel like sticking him back." It is all right to feel as if he might like to stick the doctor back, even though he would not be permitted to do so. Third, it helps prevent any misconception that the youngster has about losing a large amount of blood which could be dangerous to him.

Other procedures can scare children. A child might be frightened by the process of having an X-ray taken. He may be strapped to a table or held up against an X-ray plate while an ominous-looking mechanical contraption is adjusted in various ways and a technician disappears behind an enclosure with the warning to the child, "Hold absolutely still." The child needs to be told that there is nothing here that will hurt him, and that this machine only takes a special kind of picture that helps doctors in their examination of a child.

In specialized X-ray examinations, such as those of the stomach, intestines, and urinary system, the reason that children swallow barium, have barium inserted into the rectum, or have a dye injected into a vein is to enable the doctor to see the outline of organs that would not be seen in an ordinary X-ray picture. This fact should be explained to a child in terms suited to his age. For example, a four-year-old should be told that he will be given something to drink which some people may find unpleasant and then the doctor will take a picture that will help him in his examination. A child of twelve can be given an explanation of the fact that certain organs do not show up on an X-ray because of their composition. Therefore, the doctor gives him something to drink which fills up the space within the organ and then the shape of it can be seen on an X-ray picture. When a patient is to be fluoroscoped in a dark room, he should be told about it beforehand.

Another procedure often misinterpreted by children is the electroencephalogram (or EEG). Here wires are fastened to the scalp and a recording is made of the electrical activity of the brain. Children may feel that electricity is being put into their brain which may change them in some way. The child should be given a suitable explanation. A three- or four-year-old should be told that this will not hurt him. The six- or seven-year-old can be told that this machine is not putting electricity or anything else into his brain. Children of this age and older can be told that the body's cells produce a tiny amount of electricity and that the electroencephalograph machine can make a graph, or "picture," of the activity produced by the brain, a graph which is called an EEG. We can also tell them that doctors can make a record of the electricity produced by the heart, which is called an electrocardiogram, or EKG. The doctor will look at the graph of the brain or heart activity and this, like the other parts of the examination, will help the doctor to see how children are getting along.

The purpose of immunization injections should be explained to children. Here, too, the youngsters should be told that the shots hurt a little, but the medicine that the doctor is giving them helps their body to protect them against germs that could make them sick.

In general, we should be alert to the possibility that the child may have illogical concerns about even the simpler parts of a medical examination. It would be well to ask him if he has any questions about the instruments used or why the doctor does certain things. Then proceed to answer his questions and correct his misconceptions.

For instance, a five-year-old may fear that when a doctor places an otoscope in the child's nose or ears he may be damaging them. The youngster should be told that the physician's instrument is only a specially shaped flashlight for looking into small spaces and will in no way injure him.

Some children are apprehensive because of the pressure on their arm when the blood-pressure cuff of the sphygmomanometer is pumped up. A child should be told beforehand that there will be a tight feeling on his arm and that he may feel uncomfortable for a short time while the doctor is measuring his blood pressure. He should be assured that nothing is being done to his blood.

If a child is frightened of the stethoscope, we can tell him that it is simply a tube through which the doctor hears the sounds of the heart and lungs better. This instrument makes it possible for the doctor to hear just as well as he would if he put his ear against the child's chest. The preschool-age youngster should be reassured that nothing is going into him through the stethoscope tubing.

Psychiatry

"But I don't want to go see a psychiatrist. I'm not nuts. Do you think I'm crazy?"

PUBLIC ATTITUDES about psychiatry have changed markedly in the past twenty-five years. There has been a greater acceptance of the fact that consulting a psychiatrist should not be considered different from seeking the services of any other medical specialist.

For some segments of our population, psychiatrists serve the function of a new priesthood. The words of the doctor are for certain people like pronouncements from on high. Some psychiatrists may act as if they were destined to play such a role, but most know that they are not ordained to perform as ministers of a new secular religion.

How can we view psychiatry and the need for help? I am of the opinion that we can assume all people have emotional problems. Since we share the attributes of the human condition, all of us must find adequate ways of dealing with the anxieties caused by the daily experiences of life. When we do not find relatively comfortable methods of handling our tensions, and when we do find ourselves unduly agitated or depressed, or when our behavior is very unsettling to those closely related to us, we may need professional help.

There are certain mistaken notions held by people relative to psychiatric treatment. Some come to the doctor expecting him to have a magic formula designed to straighten out all their problems quickly, or to be able to tell them exactly what to do. Others anticipate existing in a state of continuous happiness after having gone through therapy. A number of individuals even feel it is possible for man to become perfect, and that with proper treatment they can reach this goal.

Of course, none of these things is true. What the psychiatrist can do, hopefully, is aid a person to be able to see himself better and to acquire a better understanding of himself and how he functions. Along with this, the patient can have the opportunity of exercising his feelings in relation to the doctor, and thereby find more advantageous ways of controlling his emotions. When these objectives are accomplished, a person will be in a better position to develop new methods of managing his problems or to decide whether or not he even wants to change his accustomed manner of coping with his existence.

Children will on occasion request that their parents get help for them. Generally, however, it is the parent who becomes uncomfortable about the child's actions. Often parents may put up with, or overlook, unusual conduct on the child's part and may avoid seeking advice and help until the school personnel or other authorities bring the matter to their attention.

When psychiatric consultation is to be sought, parents ask how they should explain the visit and the psychiatrist's function to their youngster. The child can be told that he is to be taken to see a doctor who is different from other doctors he has seen in that this doctor does not give shots and does not examine with medical instruments. It is this doctor's job to talk and play with children and sometimes, if a child has troubles or worries, the doctor may be able to figure out ways to help him. What they talk about will just be between the child and the doctor.

The youngster who is told that he is going to see a psychiatrist may say, "Why do I have to go? I'm not crazy. Do you think I'm crazy?"

Parents should recognize that, frequently, children have such thoughts even if they do not verbalize them. We can tell the child that many people go to see psychiatrists and very, very few are what anyone would call crazy. We should let him know that we certainly do not think he is crazy, but as good parents we must seek advice in order to help with his or the family's problems. If he had a stomach ache we would take him to the proper doctor, and if there are other difficulties we are obliged to see to it that he gets help.

Unfortunately, the visit to the doctor sometimes occurs after a long period of bickering and recrimination between the parents and their child. At times the youngster has been threatened with, "I'll have to take you to a psychiatrist if you don't straighten out," or, "If your behavior doesn't improve we'll have to send you to a special school or a hospital."

If such interchanges have occurred, there will be a greater problem in getting the child to accept the recommendation of psychiatric consultation and help. It may be necessary for the parents to explain that their previous statements were spoken in the heat of anger, and it is important for the family to get outside help in order to find better ways of getting along with one another.

Many parents want to know what a child psychiatrist actually does. This varies with the individual doctor and also depends on the particular patient. Older children, and occasionally younger ones too, utilize their time with the psychiatrist to discuss their inner feelings and problems and gain insight into their own ways of functioning. Younger children may engage in fantasy play and through the medium of such activity work out their difficulties. Some gain a great deal from the undivided attention they are receiving. The psychiatrist may play games with the child. By observing the young patient's behavior while engaged in this activity and interpreting it to him, the doctor may enable the youngster to understand himself and his interaction with others better.

Most doctors tell the child that what he talks about will be kept in confidence. Parents frequently ask whether the child is "opening up" in talking to the psychiatrist, or how he is doing in his therapy sessions. The important criterion of what is being accomplished with psychotherapy is not what is happening with the doctor, but how the young patient is functioning in his everyday life, including schoolwork, his interpersonal relationships, and his management of his emotions in general.

Watching Our Language

The girl returned to her classroom from the school doctor's office. With tears in her eyes she went up to the teacher and said, "I'm upset. I've got a disease and I want to go home."

The teacher was unable to learn from the child what disease it was, but finally noted that on the card given the child, opposite the word "Illness," was written, "Obesity."

THIS YOUNG lady was actually terribly upset by the doctor's report. Fortunately, after seeing the card the teacher asked the student if she knew what "Obesity" meant, which of course she did not. The girl quickly calmed down when the teacher told her that this was the doctor's way of saying that the student was overweight.

On one occasion I saw a nine-year-old girl for psychiatric consultation because she had suddenly become unusually depressed. It developed that she was afraid she had a serious illness. A few days before, she had been to her pediatrician for a routine checkup. After the examination the doctor, speaking to the mother, who happened to be a nurse, stated that her daughter had "conjunctivitis." Naturally the mother was not upset at hearing this word. The child, however, wondered what this terrible condition could be, but asked no questions.

When the child was told by me that it simply meant she had a slight infection of her eye, and that it had already cleared up, she was greatly relieved. Her mother had no inkling of what had made the girl so anxious and depressed. She readily agreed that in the future she and the physician should avoid the use of medical terminology in the child's presence until they also explained it to the girl.

Adults, especially physicians, should watch their language. It would be better with all patients, but particularly with children, to use words that are simple and not frightening. We are often unaware that a child has overheard conversation between the parent and doctor and then drawn a completely erroneous conclusion about things. When a physician wants to tell the parent something that he prefers the child not hear, care should be taken to do this out of earshot of the young patient. Hopefully, this will be done in such a manner that the child does not become suspicious that something is going on behind his back.

The physician should give explanations to children in words that they can understand. If he does not, the parent should ask him to do so. Often information is given to the young patient and he really does not comprehend what he has been told. He may be afraid or ashamed to ask questions about it for fear that he will appear stupid. (This is sometimes true for adult patients too.) It is well for the parent and doctor to ask the child if he has any questions about the explanation which he has been given. We should try to determine whether or not the child has actually understood.

Children may be frightened, and although they are given an explanation about their medical condition, they may not absorb the information. In such instances it is necessary to repeat again later what has been told to them.

For example, a nine-year-old boy was ill with diarrhea and vomiting. He was told that it was caused by food poisoning and that he would soon feel well. He did recover but seemed very upset. Later it was discovered that he really did not understand what was meant by food poisoning. He thought someone had put poison into his food and that it would happen again.

It was then explained to him that when certain foods are not kept at the proper temperature, germs may grow in the food and spoil it. Spoiled food made him sick, not a poison that was purposely put into his food. He was told that he had recovered and would not have further trouble from this particular illness.

Going to the Hospital

"What's going to happen when I go to the hospital, Mommy?"
"I don't know, dear, we'll find out when we get there."
"But, Mommy, I want to know now!"

YES, CHILDREN do want to know. They may not always verbalize their concerns, but it is safe to assume that they are wondering about what is going to happen to them.

Perhaps there are still parents who are so uncomfortable with their child's reaction to unpleasant things that they hesitate to be truthful with them. This certainly is not the course to follow. It is far better to put up with a child's tearful response than to have him feel that he has been tricked.

What does happen to a child who goes to the hospital for an operation? The parent and child arrive at the hospital, and from there on the procedure varies from one hospital to another. Usually they are interviewed by a receptionist as to name, address, age, or other routine information (including perhaps his nickname, favorite toys, and the words he uses for routines such as toilet procedures).

After this, laboratory work may be performed. This involves sticking the child's finger and withdrawing a few drops of blood; or a small amount of blood (equal to about a teaspoonful) may be collected in a syringe by inserting a hypodermic needle into one of the child's veins. A specimen of urine is usually collected.

The young patient is then taken to his room or ward. Here he undresses and puts on hospital clothing or his own pajamas. Certain routine procedures are then carried out: a nurse takes his temperature, pulse, and perhaps blood pressure; an intern examines the patient; and in some instances an enema may be given. For a period of time before the operation, food is withheld from the child.

The procedures for anesthetizing children vary in different hospitals. For example, in the Children's Hospital of the District of Columbia there is a playroom in the operating suite. The children come in on the morning of the operation and play in the playroom for fifteen to thirty minutes. Adjacent to the playroom are two rooms where the process of anesthesia is started. The child comes in together with his parents and the child is put to sleep by the anesthetist using an odorless gas, nitrous oxide, which is administered through a mask. The patient is then taken into the operating room where the anesthesia is continued with other anesthetic substances.

In other good hospitals, the parents and the young patient may be interviewed by the anesthesiologist the day before the operation. The doctor will ask about any past anesthetic experiences and whether or not the child has any allergies of sensitivities to particular drugs. He will also explain to the child what type of anesthetic he will be receiving, for example, if he will have a needle injected into a vein or if he will be given an anesthetic gas through a mask. The next day, the child may receive some premedication about thirty minutes before the operation. This could be given by mouth or by injection. In some instances the medication may be given rectally. Some children, especially if they are over ten years of age, may possibly be given an intravenous injection to start the anesthesia. The anesthetist will take the child from his room to the operating room where the anesthesia will be continued, and the operation will be performed. The main aftereffect of anesthesia in children will be nausea.

When the operation is complete, the patient is usually taken to a "recovery room" until he awakens. Then he is put back into his own hospital room, where he remains during his hospitalization.

The amount of preparation required for this experience of hospitalization and operation varies with the individual child. He should feel that the operation is a necessary thing, and this may best be done by talking it out or playing it out. The information should come, if possible, from someone the child relies upon and trusts.

For the two- to four-year-old patient a statement from the parent that the procedure should be done, and the reassurance that everything will be all right may be all that is needed. If a four-year-old is very bright and asks more questions about what will be happening to him, we should certainly give him truthful answers. The five-year-old or older child should be given more information about what will happen to him in the hospital. He may not be able to understand or utilize everything that is told to him, but he will have an idea of what is to happen. With the school-age child it would be a good plan to give him the information a week or two before the operation. Permit him to talk over his fears, reassure him, and correct any misconceptions about the anticipated event.

Playing out the situation beforehand may be valuable. The child can be encouraged to go through the coming events step by step, using a doll or toy animal as the subject. In this way he may be able to express and get rid of some of his feelings about the coming operation. Some hospitals actually conduct tours for children to familiarize them with the setting. For instance, in the Children's Hospital of the District of Columbia, youngsters who are to undergo certain types of elective surgery are taken through the hospital beforehand. Also, groups of school children are taken on tours of parts of the hospital.

If a child desires to take some tangible object from home, a toy or an article of clothing, he should be permitted to take it. In fact, it might be a good policy to give him the opportunity to take "a little bit of home" with him.

You should avoid the use of frightening terms when discussing an anticipated hospitalization with a child. It would be advisable to find out in what ways the situation at your hospital differs from what has been outlined here. Explain to your child why you may not be with him at a certain point, and assure him that you will visit him as soon as you are permitted to do so.

Upon his return home from the hospital, the child should be permitted to "talk over" how he felt about his experience, and we should attempt to correct any mistaken notions he might have about what happened, especially to him.

Should Parents Stay?

"Should I stay here at the hospital with my son?" the mother asked the nurse.

"You really don't need to," was the reply. *"They usually behave better when the parents aren't here."*

PARENTS OFTEN ask whether or not it is best for them to be with their child during the hospital stay. Some enlightened hospital administrations have made provisions for rooming-in by the parents during the time of their child's hospitalization. Many have provided for extremely liberal visiting privileges for parents. Others still have very limited visiting hours. But even where the hospital policy is liberal, some of the personnel tend to discourage parents from staying on the basis of the notion that the children "behave" better when their parents are not around.

The meekest child, the one who objects least to what is being done to him and who shows the least emotion about his hospitalization, is probably not the child who is making the best adjustment to his situation. He may likely be the child who will carry with him from the hospital some undesirable and unnecessary emotional problems.

Children have certain fears attached to the business of going away from home to the hospital. Younger children, and to some extent older ones too, fear the separation from their parents and from the security that the parents represent. As discussed elsewhere in this book, separation anxiety is an emotion that we all experience sometime in life. It can be greatly accentuated in a child, particularly a younger one, when he has to be subjected to the new and frightening experience of a hospital stay.

Very young children, whose parents are not permitted to stay with them at the hospital, may feel that they have been abandoned. They may cry a lot and become depressed.

The mother should be with the young child as much as possible during the period of hospitalization. Older children too benefit from regular visits by their parents. The presence of his mother and father is reassuring to the patient, and he can have the opportunity to voice any concerns he has about what is happening to him.

There is another consideration. It would be wonderful if we could feel that hospital care is excellent in every respect; however, this is not always the case.

We should not interfere with our child's medical care by telling the physician how to treat our youngster. But often things ordered by the doctor are left undone. The child may be wet and need to be cleaned up. He may be in pain or uncomfortable and be unable to ask for help or necessary medication. Similar things happen to adult patients, but they are more resourceful in getting the attention of the ward personnel than the child patient. If the parents are present they can be instrumental in bringing to the notice of the hospital staff the things that are not being done properly in relation to their child.

Too frequently, not enough attention is paid to the patient even when hospital staff is adequate, and often hospitals are understaffed these days. We should not simply assume that a youngster is cranky and complaining for no good reason until we have made sure that his complaints do not have some basis in fact.

Is there any reason why a parent should not stay with a child, even though the hospital rules permit it? Other than realistic considerations such as having other children unattended at home, there is one situation where the parent's staying might be questioned. If a parent is so uncomfortable with the idea of the child's hospitalization and the necessary procedures that will be carried out, it may be readily noticed by the child. The parent's anxiety may be communicated to the child, causing the young patient to be even more disturbed. In such circumstances it is advisable for the other parent, or a family member who is well known to the child, to be there with him.

Scheduling Elective Surgery

"Ronald needs to be circumcised," said Dr. Roberts, "and this seems like a good time to do it."

"But, Doctor," said Ronald's mother, "does it have to be done now? He's been so fearful lately."

CERTAIN OPERATIONS are emergencies. For example, if appendicitis is diagnosed an operation cannot be postponed. There is often little time to prepare a child, under these circumstances, for the experience of hospitalization.

We must do what we can, in the interval available to us, to tell the youngster as much as we know about what is going to happen to him, and try to answer any questions he may ask. We should assure him that the operation must be done as soon as possible, and render him as much support as we can. We really cannot stop to give very much consideration to the stage of personality development that the child is going through, or to the fact that he is showing signs of emotional upset unrelated to the operation.

Other operations, however, are not emergencies and are spoken of as "elective surgery." In these situations the surgical procedure is necessary, but does not have to be done immediately. In scheduling these operations parents and their physician should consider the stage of development of the child, and any evident signs of emotional disturbance.

There are particular periods when it would be advisable to postpone any elective surgery. In normal development, during the latter half of the first year of life the infant becomes fearful of being separated from his mother. Simultaneously the baby becomes afraid of strangers, and this is a time when operations that are not urgent should be postponed. This would be especially true in any hospital with no provision for the mother to sleep in the room, or at least be permitted to remain in the room with the infant.

During the period that the younger child is involved with working out the fears about bodily damage, we should be hesitant to expose him to any operation that is not an emergency. Evidence that he may be having a problem with this stage of development may take the form of fears he develops of various animate or inanimate objects. Or he may be waking up with bad dreams, often relating to an imagined animal in his bed, or room, with him.

Specific events occurring in the life of a child and his family should give us pause when we consider subjecting the youngster to elective surgery. When a new sibling has recently arrived, the child has to handle a whole range of feelings toward his parents and the new baby. Other happenings that produce special problems are the death of a person who has had a close relationship with the child and his family, or recent illness in a parent or sibling. If a father's job involves periodic travel away from home, it would be advisable to schedule the operation in a space of time during which Dad will be at home both before and after the hospitalization.

These are some of the factors to be considered in scheduling elective surgery. Do not hesitate to bring them up and discuss them with your physician. While surgery may be "elective," there can be limits to how long one should wait. Your doctor will be the one to make this judgment, but he will have no way of knowing what else may be involved for the family unless it is brought to his attention.

Fears of Younger Children

Three-year-old Billy was scheduled to go to the hospital for a hernia operation. He remembered that his mother re-

64 What Shall We tell the Kids?

cently came back from the hospital after giving birth to his baby sister.

"Mommy," he asked, "when I go to the hospital will they take my wee-wee off like they did with the baby?"

THE CONCERN expressed by Billy is a common one in childhood. In the course of normal development, youngsters go through a stage in which they become very concerned that part of their body will be hurt. This occurs usually between the ages of one and a half and four years.

During this period children may develop fears of various kinds. They become afraid of dogs and other animals, vacuum cleaners, thunder, lightning, loud noises, and many other things. What they are basically worried about is that some part of their body will be hurt. They need to be told that these animate or inanimate objects will not hurt them in any way. Some of the same fear comes up again in adolescence, but not in such a direct form. The teen-ager shows it in his hypochondriacal tendencies.

Sometimes the fear is present before a child can verbalize it. On a visit to a friend's home a fifteen-month-old boy, who was not talking yet, became terrified of a toy cow that lifted its head and said "Moo." After this initial frightened reaction he would never enter that room until he was assured that the toy had been put away. When the boy was about two years of age and had begun to talk he mentioned his friend's cow. His father questioned him, asking, "What about the cow?" "I'm afraid," he answered. "What are you afraid of?" asked his parent. "It's going to bite my finger off," the child replied. Before he had developed the ability to express himself verbally, he had experienced this threat to the integrity of his body.

When a child begins to have this fear he often finds evidence to prove that there is reason to be afraid. If he has a sister and has seen her undressed, he notices that, compared to him, something is missing in her genital area. He may say to his parents, "What happened to Mary's peepee?" A little girl who saw her brother's penis asked her mother, "When will I have a penis again?" The female child may believe that part of her is gone and that perhaps further damage will occur. The boy is afraid that he will lose a part of his body, the way that his sister did.

At the time that a child verbalizes his concern about possible bodily damage, or in some other way asks about the difference between male and female genitalia, the parent is presented with an opportunity to tell the youngster that girls and boys are born different, that girls never had a penis. Girls grow up to be women and can become mothers, and boys grow up to be men and can become fathers. Even if a young child does not openly express these concerns, parents would be wise to maintain an awareness that these misconceptions frequently exist. The parents should look for opportune moments to supply information and reassurance to their offspring.

If a child who is having these worries about his body needs an operation, he will bring these concerns with him to the hospital. Children sometimes imagine that something was done to their body while they were asleep, and they fear that the damage will increase after the operation is completed. Some may misinterpret the operation and believe that it is in reality a punishment.

Children may believe that they are changed in such a way that they are not as they were before, or not like other chilren, and that they are not able to do the things they previously did. All these feelings, coupled with a lack of preparation of the child, may lead to evidence of emotional upsets, sometimes showing up in the form of persistent fears, uncomfortable habits, or changes in attitudes or behavior. For example, a child may develop a fear of the dark, or of going to sleep at night, or a fear of leaving home. A child may regress in his toilet habits, may change his eating habits, or develop a tic of some kind. A child who has been fairly aggressive may become very timid.

These are the reasons for making an attempt to prepare a

youngster for the experience of going to the hospital for an operation. The parent should explain what is going to happen to the child in the particular operation that he will have. The type of explanation should be in keeping with the age of the young patient.

With the most common operations of childhood, such as the tonsillectomy and hernia repair, the child should be assured that he will be no different than he was before. If an operation is performed that produces a noticeable change, he should be told what the change will be and assured that nothing else will be changed. For example, if a child has an injury to his finger and part of it must be removed, he may imagine that more of his finger will disappear even after the operation. He should be told specifically *what* will be removed and that, once the operation is over, nothing else is going to happen to his hand.

When a child has any operation that involves visible sutures, or stitches, he may fear that when the stitches are removed the wound will break open. He may believe that it is the stitches that are holding him together. He should be told that the stitches are only a temporary help to hold the edges of the cut, or wound, together. Nature sees to it that the body heals the wound; then when the skin is again strong enough to stay together, the stitches are removed.

Occasionally, two operations will be done on a patient at the same time to avoid giving anesthesia twice. Unless this is explained to the child beforehand, difficulties can arise. One little boy continued to cough for a long time after a tonsillectomy. No physical cause for the symptom could be found. A psychiatrist who eventually saw the boy discovered that the child had not been told at the time of the operation that he was going to be circumcised along with having his tonsils removed. With his own "logic," the boy had concluded that since his throat was sore, the missing foreskin of his penis had been put in his throat, and he was trying to cough it out.

If more than one operative procedure is to be performed at the same time, this should be explained to the patient. As always, let us remember that we should try to learn from the child what his questions, worries, and misconceptions are so that we can help him to deal with his problems. A parent can ask a child, "What do you think is going to happen to you?" What we specifically tell a child will depend on what his concerns are. If the child's questions cannot be answered from the material presented here, a parent should get the necessary information from the child's physician.

Tonsillectomy and Adenoidectomy

The doctor examined Susie's throat and then turned to her mother and said, "Susie's tonsils and adenoids should come out. We'll schedule her for the operation."

When the doctor left the room Susie asked her mother, "What are tonsils, what's an operation, what are they going to do to me?"

TONSILLECTOMY is the most common operation of childhood; it is often the child's first experience with hospitalization. Usually when this operation is performed it is accompanied by an adenoidectomy, the removal of the adenoids.

Children should be given accurate information in keeping with their age. Parents need to know something about the subject in order to explain things to their children.

What are tonsils and adenoids? Tonsils are rounded formations of what is called lymphoid tissue, and they are located on both sides of the rear portion of a person's mouth cavity. This part of the body is called the pharynx. The adenoids are also collections of this type of lymphoid tissue, and are located in the upper part of a space that exists behind the nose passages. The tonsils and adenoids reach their largest size during childhood and begin to decrease in size during puberty.

Why are tonsils and adenoids sometimes removed? If adenoids become too enlarged, certain problems can result. There may be obstruction of the nasal passageways. Children then may have trouble breathing, develop a nasal quality to their voice, have a high arching of the palate, and possibly malocclusion of their teeth. Another serious consequence that large adenoids can cause is the blocking of the Eustachian tube which leads to the ear. Middle-ear infections then lead to impaired hearing.

Large tonsils may produce difficulty in swallowing. Tonsils may have to be removed because of repeated attacks of infection which sometimes produce an abscess around the tonsil. Recurrent or persisting swollen glands in the neck may be another reason for recommending tonsillectomy.

What does the doctor actually do when he removes a patient's tonsils and adenoids? After the child is anesthetized the surgeon takes hold of the tonsil with a special instrument. He then carefully dissects (separates out) the tonsil with a sharp surgical scalpel (knife blade), and with a third instrument a wire loop is placed around the tonsil and it is removed. The doctor then makes sure that there is no excessive bleeding.

The adenoids are removed with a special instrument called an "adenotome." Again the physician will check to see that all the tissue has been removed and that bleeding has been controlled.

After the operation, the child is placed on his stomach to promote drainage of secretions from his mouth. There may be a small amount of dark, bloody material coming from his throat. Occasionally he may vomit some blood that has been swallowed. Sometimes he may experience pain in the ears, a not unusual occurrence. He should be told that there is nothing wrong with his ears.

We should answer the child's questions about his tonsillectomy. He should be told in general what will happen to him in the hospital and be given specific information, appropriate to his age, about the procedure he is to undergo. He should be told that his throat will be sore, but that essentially he will be no different after the operation than he was before. He can be informed that after a period of restricted activity, usually about one week, he will be back doing all the things that he did before.

After the operation, the parent should follow the physician's recommendations for the postoperative care of the child. If the young patient is concerned about slight bloody discharges from his mouth or throat, he should be assured that this is not unusual. Of course, if there is much bleeding, or even a question in the parent's mind, the doctor should be notified.

Hernia Repair

Freddy was very upset after his hernia repair operation. "Why didn't you tell me I was going to have this dark line on my tummy? What did they take out of me?"

A COMMON operation of childhood, especially for boys, is the hernioraphy or hernia repair.

What is a hernia? A hernia is an abnormal protrusion of any organ or tissue through any opening in the body. In common usage, however, we are usually referring to the pushing of abdominal organs through an opening in the wall of the abdomen.

The abdominal cavity and its organs are covered with a thin membrane called the peritoneum. Before birth, while the baby is developing, a pouch of this peritoneum goes along with the testicle as it moves down from the abdomen to its place in the scrotum. This pouch ordinarily becomes obliterated except for a small part which remains as a covering for the testicle. If this pouch does not become closed off, a hernia (called an inguinal hernia) may be apparent at birth or during the first few months or years of life. Hernias can also appear in older children and adults.

The symptom of an inguinal hernia is a bulging or swelling in the groin area. This swelling appears when the patient strains or cries or when he is in a standing position. It disappears when he lies down. Sometimes, along with the bulging there may be a dull discomfort.

Most of the time a hernia is what doctors call "reducible"; that is, the organs that are in the hernia sac can easily go back into the abdominal cavity. But one of the dangers of a hernia is that the organs may become stuck or "irreducible." Then it becomes a surgical emergency, for the abdominal contents cannot be returned to the abdominal cavity without an operation. A "strangulated" hernia is one where the blood supply to the herniated organ has been blocked off. This can be a dangerous situation if an operation is not carried out promptly.

What does the surgeon do when he operates on a child to repair a hernia? After the young patient is anesthetized, the doctor makes an opening through the skin using a sharp surgical knife blade. This incision usually is made along the crease of the groin. Next, the doctor divides part of an abdominal muscle and locates the pouch of peritoneum through which the abdominal organs have pushed down. He then ties off this sac and separates it so there will no longer be a space for the contents of the abdomen to push through again. The muscles and skin are sewed up and, when healing has occurred, the abdominal wall is stronger. What the child sees is the scar or "dark line" on his abdomen.

Because the location of the inguinal hernia is near the genital area, many little boys are concerned that something may happen to their penis or testicle during the operation.

They should be told what actually will be done, and they should be assured that nothing will be taken out of their body, and specifically that nothing is going to happen to their genitals after the surgery.

They can be told that they may be uncomfortable for a while following the operation, but except for the scar they will be no different than they were before. The doctor will want them to take it easy for a period of time, but afterward they will be back doing the things they previously did. They can also be told that, in time, the scar will become lighter and less noticeable.

Broken Bones and How They Heal

Jimmy had a plaster cast on his leg and a very worried look on his face.

"What's the matter, son?" asked the father.

"When they take this cast off," said Jimmy, "will my leg still be there?"

WHEN THIS young man came to the orthopedic clinic to have a cast put on his leg, he happened to see another boy who had been born without a leg. Jimmy really became concerned that he might look like that when his cast was finally removed. He needed to be assured that he had a broken bone which would heal, that he would not lose his leg, and that eventually he would be no different from the way he was before his injury.

Broken bones are common occurrences in childhood. Active boys, in particular, are going to sustain fractures jumping from high places, engaging in athletics, and being the victims of accidents of various kinds. Some children will be relatively fortunate in that, though they may need to have a cast on an extremity, their activity will not be limited completely. Others will be immobilized in bed because they need to be in traction, or they may be limited by a very large plaster cast.

The child has physical concerns about his injury, and he may also have emotional problems that were created by his accident. The physician, as a rule, is very attentive to the task of getting a good physical result in his patient, but often not attentive enough to the types of questions and concerns the youngster may have. The young patient may not be given the opportunity to ask, or may be afraid to ask, about the things that are on his mind.

It would be well for parents to have some knowledge about what a fracture is and how it heals. They would then be in a position to explain these things to their child if the physician does not do so. Parents should also be aware of some of the things children wonder about when they sustain injuries.

What is a fracture? A fracture is a break in the normal structure of a bone. Fractures are called "simple" when the skin over the bone is not broken and the bone is not exposed to air. A "compound" fracture is one in which the bone is exposed to air. A fracture can be "complete" where the two broken ends of the bone are severed all the way across, or "incomplete" where the bone has a crack in it but is not broken into two separate pieces. Such a crack is called a "greenstick" fracture. Another term one might hear in relation to fractures is "impacted" which means that the two broken ends appear to be forced up against each other. A "comminuted" fracture is a break in which the ends are broken into many pieces.

Fractures occur most often in a child's extremities. In the thigh, there is a long bone called the femur. In the lower portion of the leg are two bones, a thick bone—the tibia—and a thin bone—the fibula. The bone of the upper arm is the humerus and the forearm contains two bones, the radius and the ulna. Another bone which is frequently broken is the collar bone, or clavicle, which extends from the breastbone to the shoulder.

Another condition that can occur involving bones and joints is a dislocation. This means that one of the bones, which meets another bone to form a joint, has come out of place. When this happens a person may not be able to move his joint in the usual way, and he may experience a great deal of pain.

Once a bone is broken, how does it heal? When the bone breaks there is bleeding from the ends of the bone and from the soft tissue around the place of the fracture. The bleeding produces a large clot, called a "hematoma." This hematoma becomes infiltrated with cells that form a fibrous kind of tissue that produces a cement substance called "osteoid." Bone minerals get deposited into this soft substance forming a "callus" which is considered to be an immature form of bone and can be seen on an X-ray picture.

It is as if a bridge has been built between the two ends of the broken bone. In children this callus can usually be seen on the X-ray within three weeks of the time of the fracture. More and more minerals are deposited and the immature bone becomes converted into mature bone. The joining of the two broken ends of the bone becomes solidified, and the excess amount of callus subsequently is absorbed so that the bone regains its original shape.

What does the doctor try to do in his treatment? He tries to align the two broken ends so that the bone will eventually be straight and have the proper length. When this alignment has been accomplished, the bone must be kept in one position (immobilized) so that the healing process may go on. After the fracture has healed, the physician is concerned with the restoration of function to the injured part of the body.

Sometimes, little has to be done if the bone ends are in the proper alignment to each other, or if the break is an incomplete one. In many cases the mere application of a plaster cast will be sufficient to keep the edges of the fractured bone in the proper position for healing to occur. In other instances the fractured borders of the bone will be too far away from each other and muscle spasm may aggravate the displacement. When this situation exists, the doctor has to "reduce" the fracture by overcoming, in some way, the muscle spasm and putting the two ends of the bone in a more favorable proximity to each other. Sometimes an anesthetic may have to be given because of the pain that may be present when the reduction of the fracture is carried out.

The break may be in an area where the muscle pull is so great that any alignment the doctor could obtain would not be sustained by a plaster cast. Then traction becomes necessary. Traction is provided by putting a wire or metal pin through the bone on the far side of the fracture. In some instances an adhesive material, applied to the sides of a child's arm or leg, is used instead of the metal pin. Weights are attached to the pin (or adhesive material) and by means of pulleys a constant pull is maintained to overcome the force of the muscles that would prevent the proper bridging of the break by new bone. The traction is continued until healing has progressed to the place where the ends of the bone will not pull apart even if the weights are released. At this point a cast is usually applied.

In relatively infrequent instances, children's fractures cannot be reduced by closed manipulation or by traction and an operation has to be performed.

The restoring of function to the injured extremity is as important as any other part of the treatment. When a part of the body has been immobilized for a long time, the joints become stiff and the muscles become withered because of disuse. These things have to be corrected. At the proper time various exercises and physiotherapy are very necessary to restore adequate function of the muscles and joints.

We have gone into these matters in some detail because children do wonder about what is happening to them. With a degree of understanding about how fractures heal, parents can try to deal with the child's questions.

When children who were physically active are immobilized, they begin to notice that their muscles, which previously were firm, become flabby. They will be worried by this and should be told that this is what normally happens to anyone who is not getting regular exercise. They should be assured that when they have recovered and are running, playing, and exercising again, their muscles will become as firm as they were before the injury.

On removal of their casts, young patients will notice that the affected arm or leg will be much thinner than the opposite one. Here too, they need to be told that with proper exercises their arms and legs will regain the former size and shape.

Sometimes, children will be concerned with whether or not they will be able to do the things they did before the injury. Unless they will in some way be limited, it is important to let them know that they certainly will be able to do what they were accustomed to doing previously.

If the injury will leave a youngster handicapped in any way, this should be explained. What a child should be told depends on what the handicap will be. The parent should get the details from the physician who is caring for the child. Even if the doctor gives the child a full explanation, the young patient may want to talk to his parents about it. We can try to find out how other people with a similar handicap have compensated for it. With this information in hand, we can let our child know realistically what his possibilities and potentials are. We should be careful not to promise him things that are not possible just because we and he are upset at the bad news. We should understand that the child may justifiably feel angry when he learns that he has suffered any permanent loss of function. He will need the opportunity to express his feelings about this.

Emotional Reactions to Injury

It was the first week of summer vacation. The young teenager jumped from his skate board, and as he hit the ground, something in his thigh snapped. He knew he had broken a leg. He behaved admirably while waiting for the rescue squad, while in the emergency room of one hospital and in the process of being transferred to another hospital, and also while a metal pin was put through his leg in order that traction could be applied. But then he was told that he would be in traction in the hospital for six to eight weeks.

"I blew it," he said. "I blew the whole summer." And now he became very depressed.

THE YOUNG man involved in this accident remained bedridden and in traction for eight weeks. Following this, he was in a long leg cast for six weeks, and then on crutches for another six weeks. For an active adolescent this was a cruel fate.

In addition, he was extremely angry with himself because it was through his own actions that he was deprived of the anticipated joys and relaxation of summer. To a boy of thirteen, losing a summer most certainly would be the equivalent of his father's losing six months' income because of an injury.

Yet many of the hospital personnel could not understand why he was so depressed and angry. They may have felt that the anger was directed toward them. When the unhappy patient threw a plastic drinking cup across the room, an orthopedic resident physician put the boy on large doses of tranquillizers without first attempting to talk to the youngster about how he felt or why he felt the way he did.

The way a child reacts to a hospitalization for an operation or injury often depends on his pre-illness personality, and on what his life style has been. It is much more difficult for an active, on-the-go boy or girl to be immobilized in bed than it would be for the phlegmatic child who is content to sit and read, watch television, or engage in other sedentary activity.

Besides the concern that a child has about his physical condition when an injury occurs, emotional problems may be present. Depression occurs frequently. The young patient may be unhappy about the fact that he must remain immobile or about the life he is missing outside the hospital. He may be angry with himself because the accident was his fault. He may have feelings of guilt because he disobeyed parental rules. Many children have heard their parents say, "One of these days you're going to get hurt doing those things you do." Other children may look on their illness or injury as punishment for some indiscretion or perhaps for an "evil thought" they may have had.

Younger children can become very depressed in the hospital because of separation from their parents, especially the mother. This is particularly true in hospitals where parents are not permitted to stay overnight, and where visiting hours are not liberal.

Parents and hospital personnel who have to take care of a child must realize that it is normal for him to be depressed in these circumstances. We need to put ourself in the patient's place and try to be aware of his feelings.

If a child is angry about what has happened to him, we should tell him that most kids would feel the same way. We can sympathize with him if he says the accident would not have occurred had he done something just a little sooner or a little later than he did. Most of us would feel that way too. We can tell the child that one cannot usually anticipate accidents; and, while we should exercise care, we should not stop enjoying certain activities because a small degree of risk is involved. If we can determine that a youngster feels he has been punished for some real or imagined indiscretion, we should assure him that the injury was not a punishment.

Children react in various ways in the hospital. Some cry a great deal. We should not make them ashamed of this, rather we should make the effort to find out what thoughts or fears have caused the crying. When a child seems angry, he may be simply annoyed with himself. Nevertheless, there are occasions when physicians, nurses, aides, and orderlies have not been attentive to a patient's legitimate needs and requests, and the child may have a perfect right to be angry with them.

The child may be repetitious in his complaints and anger, and this can be quite annoying to parents. It is difficult to determine at times when to tell the child to "stop going on and on about this matter," but it is important to allow a child sufficient opportunity to rid himself of some anger, whether it is directed toward himself, hospital personnel, or fate.

Our aim should be to help young patients get over the emotional reaction to their illness or injury that landed them in the hospital. Dealing with temporary adversity can produce prolonged emotional problems for some children; but for others, as with so many things in life, it can also be a learning experience that results in positive gains for their personality development.

Hospitalization of a Parent

Hank's mother needed an operation. She didn't want her son to be upset about it, so she made plans to leave for the hospital while he was in school. Hank came home and found his mother gone.

"Where's Mom?" he asked.

He was told she went to the hospital.

"Why did she leave without telling me? Is she coming back?"

THE HOSPITALIZATION of a parent can provoke great anxiety in a child. The youngster depends on the parent to take care of him and he becomes concerned when his mother or father is ill or injured.

A child may feel sorry that his parent is ill, but he is probably more upset by the threat of the possible loss of security that his parent represents. He may also feel guilty because of hostile wishes he may sometimes have had toward the parent. The child may show signs of being disturbed if he is told that his mother or father must go to the hospital.

Parents may want to avoid seeing their child's tears and hearing the complaints about the parent going to the hospital. At times a parent will elaborately contrive to leave home while the child is in school or while he is asleep. When the child discovers that the parent is gone, he may be upset and angry.

When we need an operation several factors should be taken into account. If it is an emergency situation there is no choice. With an elective operation, however, the state of the child's development and any unusual family events, such as a birth or death, should be considered in determining whether it is a good or bad time to be absent from the home.

In any event, when hospitalization of a parent is to occur, the child should be told about it. Even in case of an emergency operation or illness requiring hospitalization, information about the parent going to the hospital should be given to the offspring. If the affected parent is unable for any reason to tell the child, the other parent or a close family member or friend should inform the youngster.

When hospitalization is not imminent, the mother should tell the child that she will be going to the hospital and approximately when she will be coming home. For the very young child it would be sufficient to make the simple statement that Mother has to go to the hospital and hopes to be back by a certain time. He should also be told who will take care of him in his mother's absence. An older child can be given more complete information about what will happen to the parent.

A youngster may ask his mother (or father) what kind of operation she is going to have? Is it dangerous? Will she die? The parent should explain as much as she can about what will be done to her. She can tell the child that nowadays operations are safe even though Mother may not feel very well for a few days after the operation. She will get better after that. If a probably fatal condition exists, the child may have to be told that there is a possibility that the parent may not recover, but that the doctors will do everything they can to get the parent well.

When Mother goes to the hospital for the delivery of another baby, the child is faced with two situations—the mother's absence for a period of time and her return with a new infant who will likely be viewed as an interloper and competitor. At times the parent may go into labor in the middle of the night. In most instances it is a good idea to awaken the child, tell him Mother is going, and let him know who will stay there with him.

A parent should explain to younger children that the hospital does not permit visits by them because of their age. It is well to tell them that you will talk to them on the phone as soon as you are permitted to do so.

With younger children, be prepared for various reactions on your return from the hospital. Some children may be angry because of a feeling that they have been abandoned; initially, they may be reluctant to look at you, talk to you, or even acknowledge the fact that you have returned. Others may cling to you and not want to let go, afraid that you will leave again.

Try to understand what the child is feeling and what he

may be saying with his words and actions. If for medical reasons the child is not to climb on your lap or if other precautionary measures must be taken, you should explain to him that you love him very much and missed him while you were gone, but the doctor does not want anyone to climb on Mother now, and that he can sit close by you.

Often, at times when a child has the greatest need to be heard and understood, he is shunted off by well-meaning relatives. In their effort to spare the parent, they forget that the child is also having problems with his feelings. These relatives should realize that the child's feelings are very important on these occasions. They should spend more time with the youngster and tell him that while they know how much he would like to be near his mother, Mother needs more time to rest and recover. They should not make the child feel ashamed if he becomes angry about this.

The Fatally Ill Child

Steven was getting worse. He had bone cancer and it was spreading all through his frail body.

Some members of the hospital staff, who used to stop by and visit frequently, came less often. One of them was asked why this was so.

"It makes me so sad to see him suffering," she replied, "so I try to avoid coming into his room."

THE ATTITUDE of this nurse's aide was unfortunate but understandable. For most of us, to think of children being ill is an uncomfortable thought, but to think of their suffering and dying is almost unbearable. Yet, a few children do develop fatal diseases and they need special care.

Very few happenings in life are more heartrending to a parent than the knowledge that his child has a terminal illness. The staggering fact of the impending death of one's offspring will tremendously disturb the emotional well-being of the most mature and stable parent.

For health care personnel the problem is also a formidable one. They, as well as the parents, will be plagued by an agonizing feeling of helplessness. The physician, who earnestly desires that the child get well, will know that our present state of medical knowledge offers no answers in the case of the particular disease involved. The doctor, perhaps, will have to struggle with his own unreasonable feelings of guilt for not being able to do more.

The situation that presents itself is distressing and depressing to all concerned, and because this is so, it produces a set of circumstances that tend to make it difficult to supply what the dying patient needs. For he requires the support and presence of people to whom he feels close, and on whom he is dependent for his care.

We who are physicians, nurses, and other paramedical personnel should be aware of how we feel. We should admit to our feelings of helplessness and try to deal with them. We should face our anger and recognize "that no one knows why this had to happen to a blameless child." But we must remember that the fact that we are uncomfortable is not a justifiable reason for avoiding the child. A young patient may not realize the seriousness of his condition, but when people who previously visited frequently either cease coming or seldom come in, the youngster may wonder if he has done something wrong or he may realize there is something terribly wrong with him.

The parents whose child has been stricken with a fatal illness have an almost impossible job to do. On the one hand, they must deal with their own feelings: the depression they will experience on hearing the diagnosis and the grief they will have; the anger they may feel that this had to happen to their child; and, at times, the guilt if they unjustifiably berate themselves for so many different things.

On the other hand, in the midst of having to cope with all their own feelings, the parents must think of their child and what must be done for him. They must summon their resources at a time when they least feel like doing so, and proceed to do what is necessary to help their ailing youngster. Parents should also be aware of the fact that in no way could they have prevented the incurable illness.

The fatally ill child needs to have hope. He needs to be told that his illness is not his fault. It did not occur because he "went out without his boots," "didn't eat the proper food," or "didn't get enough rest." A disease is not a punishment for bad acts or thoughts on his part.

As the illness progresses the child will have less energy and he will have to be more dependent. He can benefit from the continued presence and attention of the people he has come to depend upon: his parents, his doctors, the nurses and aides on the ward. The child may not feel like talking to them, but he will know that they are there.

Sometimes a young patient seems to want to talk about his fear of dying. He may say this directly or he may communicate it in other ways. Often, we get the message, but we may feel too uncomfortable to discuss his feelings with him and we avoid doing so. Although I would not recommend telling a child that he is going to die, we should permit him to talk about his feelings and fears. We can listen and we can tell him that everyone has similar fears, and we can assure him by our words and actions that we are doing everything we can to help him.

When a child is fatally ill, we might change our ways of handling him insofar as limits that are imposed and other family rules. We should be wary of how we go about this and consider whether or not the changes are wise. If marked differences are suddenly noticed by the child, he may suspect that something is terribly wrong. We can encourage him to do as much as he is able to do, and try to treat him in as similar a manner as possible to the way he has always been treated.

If there are other siblings in the family, we must be mindful of their needs and feelings. What information they should be given depends on their age and level of maturity. An explanation should be given to the children as to why their parents have to be away from them for periods of time.

Sibling rivalry is an ever-present fact. The sisters and brothers of the sick child should be told that none of their behavior, none of their angry words, thoughts, or wishes, and none of the blows they may have struck were in any way responsible for their sibling's illness. If they ask about the possibility of their sibling's dying, they can be told that while everyone dies someday, the doctors are doing everything possible to help the child. They should be assured that their sibling's condition is not hereditary and not contagious, and that they will not develop the same illness.

In discussions of incurable diseases the question arises, "Is it justified to subject a patient to the discomfort and annoyance of therapy that at best can only prolong his life for a short while?" Each set of parents will have to make this decision. I have thought of this question often and my answer would be "Yes." It may be painful for the child and the parents to put up with all that is involved, but we should remember that we never know when cures for illnesses will be found. If the patient is alive, there is still hope. People who were barely surviving with diabetes when insulin was discovered lived healthier and longer lives afterward.

CHAPTER III

Education

College Entrance

"Doctor, I'm so upset," said Mrs. Williams. *"The letters came yesterday and we didn't get into the college of our choice."*

"Who didn't get in?" asked the doctor.

THIS CONVERSATION is the end product of a process that began a long time ago. It involves the whole concept of what education is all about today. How do we affect our children's attitudes toward scholarship? And what should we try to tell them in our words and actions about education?

So often parents react as if they personally, rather than their children, have been denied admission to a particular college. They become depressed and act as if a terrible catastrophe has occurred.

We might surmise from the behavior of many people that the sole purpose of attending school for twelve years is to get into the college of one's choice, usually an Ivy League college. Parents of a child starting kindergarten will say they must make financial sacrifices and get their offspring into the best private school so that he will be accepted by a good college. They do not say that they are doing this so that the youngster will be well educated, but rather for college admission.

What is education? And when should we begin to be concerned about education?

Education begins in the cradle. Probably from the moment the infant is first held by his mother he begins to learn about the world. Too frequently, when we think of our child's educational process we tend to forget that the most important and influential educators our youngster will ever have are his mother and father. Before he attends nursery school or kindergarten, he has learned a tremendous amount from his parents, and he will continue to learn from them for years.

Children acquire knowledge from their parents in so many ways; from what we tell them and from what we do not tell them; from the things we do and from the things we do not do; from how we seem to feel and from how we make them feel. They obtain information from us in many obvious ways and also in many subtle ways.

Few of us consciously stop to think about how much our children are learning from us. Yet, what they learn in terms of our values and our attitudes toward life will exceed in importance any of the facts they will collect in their formal education.

When our offspring are ready for school, we want them to go to a good school. Advertisements remind us to set aside money for their future training. In our larger cities, private schools have been in a seller's market because the public schools are not "good enough." We want our youngsters to have excellent teachers, and we become very upset when instructors do not meet our expectations.

But we tend to forget that our children's education for coping with life rests with us. It would be well for all of us to pay attention to this most important aspect of our child's educational experience.

Let us get back to the mother who was so upset when her son did not get into the college of "our" choice. Today, young people are subjected to ridiculous pressures relative to gaining entrance to college. Instead of a logical progression in the process of their education, college becomes a symbol of status or the lack of status.

A good part of a student's time is taken up with endless testing, the filling out of applications, the writing of meaningless essays, going to visit colleges, and being interviewed by traveling administrators from the universities or by alumni representatives in the community. The student worries about whether this or that factor or activity will help or hurt his chances for admission. Grades become important not as indicators of how much one may have learned, but only for how they affect one's rank in class.

Because of their positions, all adults working with students —admission officers, counselors, teachers, and principals— tend to make more out of college-admission procedures than need be. There are so many disadvantages to the present state of affairs related to applying for college that we, as parents, should adopt an attitude that will deemphasize the import of whether a young person gets into his number-one college choice or his safety school. Anyone who has bothered to observe will readily note how many students are unhappy at their "first-choice" school. Others, who find themselves attending a third, fourth, or fifth choice, are often delighted with their university experience.

College students tell me it would be well for those attending high school to know that, once they get to the campus, the particular college matters little. Wherever students go they will always find people as bright or brighter than themselves. But, regardless of what you say to a high school senior, he will still be disappointed in a third- or fourth-choice school, because of the pressure of his peer group and other factors in the community.

Nonetheless, we should still tell children that, in the sum total of their lives, which college they attend will rarely be "that important." Very few people ever learn as much as there is to be learned at any university. Only infrequently does anyone consulting a lawyer, physician, or engineer ask him what college he attended or even where he received his postgraduate training. What a person accomplishes after he has graduated will be of more consequence than the fact that he attended a particular college.

We should maintain an attitude that will help convince our youngsters that the factor of primary importance is to become well educated. Where this is accomplished is a secondary consideration. If, for whatever reason, a student wants to apply to a specific school he should not be discouraged from doing so. But we must make it clear from the beginning that no tragedy has occurred if he is refused admission. A qualified student should be able to find a suitable college to attend and should be able to receive a good education there.

Payment for Grades

Johnny came home with his report card. He had been promised a dollar for every A and fifty cents for each B.

His father looked at the report card and with a big smile on his face said, "Johnny, you make me feel very proud and happy. Here's four dollars for your four As and one dollar for your two Bs."

THERE ARE several things wrong with what is going on between this boy and his father. Many parents pay their children for getting good grades in school; in rare instances such incentives are justified, but generally this type of reward for academic effort is a poor idea.

When it comes to education we are much better off if we stress the acquisition of knowledge as the primary purpose of learning. It is probably utopian to wish that a genuine love of learning could be instilled in every youngster and grades be done away with completely. Perhaps an effort should be made to eliminate the present grading system at least in the elementary school years.

Most children do not want to do poorly in school. Unless they are having problems of some sort they do not want to fail or behave in any other manner that would make them feel inferior. If a student is failing, we should take notice and try to determine what is going on. Does he have any physical defect that may be responsible for his learning disability? Is he having trouble seeing the blackboard and does he need glasses? Is he having a hearing difficulty? Does he have any mild neurological problem that has gone undetected? There are many possibilities of a physical nature which should be considered when a child is failing in school.

In addition to the physical causes for lack of success, emotional problems can be responsible and should be taken into account. Occasionally there may be a personality clash between an individual student and a particular teacher. Some teachers can do well with most children but seem unable to deal with a small percentage of other youngsters. It is neither the child's nor the teacher's fault; they cannot get along, and perhaps the combination of their respective makeups keeps things from working out.

At any rate, except for instances where physical problems (including intellectual deficit) or emotional disturbances interfere with proper functioning, most children make an honest effort in school.

Too frequently, students get the impression that they are not going to school and doing their homework for themselves, but rather for their parents. Their elders become very upset if their children are not doing their work or if grades are poor. A parent may say, "I'm not going to have you getting poor grades" or, "I'll have to see to it that you do your homework." In many ways the child may develop the notion, especially in the early grades, that he is working for his mother and father instead of for himself.

When a child has the idea that school is his job and he is doing it for his own benefit he is much better off. He should be told that his parents have had their schooling, and just as it is his father's function to go to work and earn a living for the family, it is the youngster's job to go to school, learn, and do the best he can for himself.

If restrictions of any type have to be imposed related to

play, television, or other activities in order that a child have time for homework, it might be done in such a manner that the child can interpret the restrictions as necessary rules for working rather than as punishments. For example, the youngster can be told that schoolwork is his obligation and it is up to him to do it. The parents cannot force him to do the work, but they can help him by seeing to it that the time and suitable atmosphere are available to him for the specific purpose of attending to his studies. The restrictions imposed, therefore, are to aid him in the process of doing his job.

To help a student by providing the proper environment for studying is fine, but to give him monetary incentives and other material inducements for doing his work is an ill-advised policy. When we do this we essentially tell a child that the purpose of learning is to gain material rewards rather than the significant compensation of gaining knowledge and developing his talent.

There is an even more important consideration for not paying children for grades. Youngsters vary in their inherited intellectual endowment. Some gifted individuals can achieve excellent marks with a minimum expenditure of energy. Others can obtain good or excellent grades only with the application of great effort. And still others can earn only average grades even though they try very hard. The student who applies himself diligently and cannot get an *A* or *B* is going to have problems related to his self-esteem. It is a cruel situation for such a child if the practice exists in his family of giving monetary rewards for high marks. He may have very able siblings who have no trouble achieving good grades. We, as parents, should attempt to gain an idea of what capabilities our children possess. We should let them know we all have strengths and weaknesses, and that we like and accept each child as he is.

The grades that a child earns *for himself* should be his reward. Certainly as parents we can be pleased when our offspring does well in his studies and we should commend him. We should not be like the father whose only comment, when his son brings home a report card with five *A*'s and a *B*, is "Why did you get that *B*?" But, while we may be pleased with our child's success, it is much more important for him to be proud of, and pleased with, himself.

The father who said to his son, "Johnny, you make me feel very proud and happy," was no doubt telling the truth. He could have made a statement which would have been better for the boy, however. He could have said, "Johnny, you can be proud of yourself for those grades." This type of pronouncement puts things where they ought to be. The job of going to school is Johnny's. His marks result from *his* efforts, and *he* will derive the benefits from his education.

Allowing an Option to Fail

"Doctor," said Mrs. Moore, "I sit with Timmy every night for several hours and I have to make him do his homework, but he's barely getting by. The school psychologist says he's average or above average in his intelligence. What should I do?"

"Let his schoolwork be up to him even if he fails," answered the physician.

"But, Doctor, what kind of a mother would I be if I did that?"

SOME CHILDREN should be given the option to fail. The whole future of a boy like Timmy can be affected by what approach we take to his schoolwork in the elementary grades.

These students who need to be exposed to a calculated risk of failure are of average or above-average intelligence, and do not have any specific learning disability. Assuming that a child fitting this description is in a class with a teacher of at least satisfactory capability, we should expect he normally would not want to fail. Under these circumstances, if a pupil is failing or barely passing in spite of a tremendous effort on the part of his parents to make him work, we must attempt to understand what might be happening.

There are, of course, many causes for school failure, but here we will take up two particular situations. In the first instance, there are students who never give the teacher much trouble. They are quiet and often unnoticed in class except perhaps for the fact that they are thought of as underachievers. These children usually do not become outwardly angry with their parents, but in having school difficulties they cause their family a good deal of trouble. The parents find themselves expending large amounts of time and energy standing over their youngsters and seeing to the carrying out of homework assignments. But there are poor results from all this effort. The children, by being so passive about the schoolwork, are acting in a very aggressive manner toward their parents.

The second type of situation is one in which parents essentially take over the responsibility for the child's success or failure in school. Frequently, this process is aided and abetted by the educational institution when the parent is called in and forcefully told, "You must do something about this child of yours. He's not working as he should." Then the homework can become the obligation of the parents rather than the youngster, and he may not concern himself about it. In essence the youngster can turn his problem over to them and feel little guilt about not doing his job.

What can we do with the child who is performing poorly because it annoys his parents, or the one who has no sense of accountability by virtue of his parents' having taken the work out of his hands? These are the children who should be given the privilege of choosing between the alternatives of success or failure.

We should tell the child that attending school is his job, and that he has not been doing it very well. He should also be told that while his parents care for him, they have decided that the course they have been following is not a good one. It is up to him to do his own work, and while his parents will be willing to explain something he doesn't understand, they will no longer police him as they formerly did. He will have a choice between passing and failing. He will be the one who determines the outcome. He has the capability to pass in school, and it is his responsibility to do so.

This is not an easy path for parents to follow. Parents feel personally embarrassed when a child fails, especially since other parents are talking about their children's wonderful academic accomplishments. For the emotional well-being of the child, however, it is well worth taking the degree of chance of failure involved; just as one takes the risks associated with a surgical operation because the alternative of not doing so is worse. We cannot sit over a student throughout all the years of his education. It is better for him to face the difficulty in the early grades, rather than push him along and have greater problems later.

If the youngster who is unconsciously using his school failure to get back at his parents finds that his work is up to him and his parents are no longer going to be unduly upset, he will probably not continue to fail. When the foregoing plan is to be followed, it is well to make arrangements with the school administrators so the child can be told that matters relevant to his school performance will be between him and his teachers.

There is a type of youngster who actually has to be anchored down to do his homework. This is the hyperactive child whose constitutional makeup is such that it is not possible for him to sit still for very long. He may present many problems for parents to deal with, school difficulty being only one of them.

The extremely active student needs more parental supervision than the average youngster. He should do his homework in a quiet place where there is a minimum number of distractions. Television and radio within his hearing distance should be turned off. He should be given only the book, paper, and pen or pencil necessary for the particular assignment. It is often helpful for one parent to be quietly present in the room where the child is working. The parent then functions as an external control for this type of child who has trouble controlling himself. If he has a relatively large amount of work to do, it would be well to break it up into smaller sections so that he might handle it without becoming too frustrated.

Teachers

"Oh, you're Bruce Eliot," said the history teacher. "I had your brother, Andy, last year and I certainly hope you're as bright as he is."

TEACHERS ARE important people in the life of a child. They can have a very positive effect, but they can also create difficulties for a student. Most of us remember a few outstanding teachers who have had a lasting influence on us. We may also recall many run-of-the-mill educators and others who actually treated us in an unfair way.

We parents will be faced with the problem of dealing with our children's attitudes about their teachers. We also will find ourselves, at times, in the position of trying to undo the harm that some unthinking teacher has done.

One type of situation often encountered by school-age children is illustrated by the history instructor's statement to Bruce. Siblings who attend the same school meet teachers who instantly compare them with favorable or unfavorable traits possessed by an older brother or sister who has preceded them. The child wants to be thought of as "me" and not as "Andy's brother."

A teacher may say to a student, "Why can't you be like your brother?" If our youngster complains to us about this, we can tell him that he can say to the teacher, "Because I'm not my brother." We should assure our son that he is not expected to be anyone but himself.

Frequently we hear statements to the effect that pupils no longer show the proper esteem for teachers. What might our attitude be, relative to this problem, and what should we tell our children about respecting educators? We may need to tell them that two elements can be involved in the question of respect for teachers. On the one hand there is the matter of respect for the position itself, and on the other, the matter of respect for the person who holds the position.

Teachers are not uniformly capable. I am acquainted with some high school students whose English teacher is so boring it is almost a daily punishment to sit through her class. It is unreasonable to expect these young people to respect this instructor on the basis of teaching ability. Nevertheless, we would be justified in asking our children to understand the teacher's limitations. We can be sympathetic to their unhappiness, or anger, in having to put up with an uninteresting and incompetent teacher. But we can also tell them that they are to respect the teacher's position and authority. They are not to use the dullness of the instruction as an excuse for unkind and disrespectful behavior toward the teacher.

Our children should be told that they will encounter a variety of teachers during their school years. We can tell them that it is their obligation to learn as much as they can from every teacher, granted that it is much easier to learn if the instructor is bright and stimulating. It is also important for children to learn to get along with different types of people.

Sometimes a child may have a teacher who is obviously

capable but who is sloughing off and doing a poor job. We can agree with our child that such a person is not doing his job and is not deserving of respect. We, rather than the youngster, should see the proper authorities and attempt to do something about the situation.

Teachers, like the rest of us, have their prejudices. They may be aware of their bias and attempt not to let it interfere with their handling of particular children. Or they may be unable to control these feelings. One sixth-grader found himself with a teacher who was known to discriminate against boys and especially against Jewish boys. This was in a public school and the teacher made a point of talking about her own religion as the right religion to believe in. Several efforts by succeeding groups of parents to have her removed from her teaching position were unsuccessful. Some parents were afraid to criticize her methods because she might then take it out on their children.

It is unjustified to expect some children to put up with, and respect, this type of person. In these circumstances, it would have been better to have certain students transferred to another class rather than endure a bigoted teacher.

In relation to their children's teachers we can find parents at both ends of a spectrum. Some maintain that the teacher is always right; others listen to their youngsters' complaints and assume that the teacher is always wrong. Of course, neither of these extreme positions should prevail. We should always listen to a child's side of a story. If there is any doubt as to the facts, we can tell him we will check to find out the teacher's view. Then we will make our decision. When the right seems to be on the child's side, we should support him. If we believe him to be wrong, we must tell him to suffer the consequences of his behavior.

There are occasions when teachers say upsetting things to young children. For instance, a second-grade teacher was in the habit of telling members of her class, "You make me so angry I want to throw you out of the window." Some of the students were greatly upset by this, even to the extent of fearing she might literally do it. If I were a parent who had the opportunity to talk to this teacher, I would tell her that what she has said would not be so bad if she would add something to it. She should follow her statement to the class with, "And sometimes you must feel angry with me and want to throw me out of the window too." Were this done, the children would get the message that she did not actually want to hurt them. She could be angry with them, and they with her, but they were all there to learn together.

If our child tells us of such an episode, we should let him know that the teacher did not mean it literally, that he, too, has a right to feel angry with the teacher. Again the right to feel angry does not give permission for actions that would actually harm the teacher.

School Phobia

It was Monday morning. Wendy, who was well the day before, complained of a stomach ache.

"I can't go to school. I feel sick," she said.

"But, dear, you don't have any fever. I think you can go," said her mother.

"I'm afraid I'll throw up in class."

"All right, Wendy, I guess you'd better stay home today."

WENDY, AFTER being permitted to remain at home, soon felt better. The pain disappeared. She played and watched television, and by three o'clock she felt well enough to go outside and play.

The next morning she again complained of abdominal pain. This time, when her mother insisted she go to school, her pain increased and she vomited. Her apprehensive mother called her physician. By the time the doctor arrived Wendy had improved and he could find nothing wrong with her.

The condition that Wendy is suffering from is usually called "school phobia." More simply it can be termed "refusal to go to school." It can begin, as it did in Wendy's case, with physical symptoms, but it can also occur as a simple refusal to go, fear of going, or near panic at the thought of going.

This pattern of behavior is different from truancy. The truant stays away from school without his parents' knowledge, occupies himself with some activity during the day, and returns home behaving as if he had attended classes. He is not frightened of the very prospect of school as is the child with school phobia who finds it necessary to stay close to home and parent during the school day.

Some relatively minor event might precipitate the youngster's refusal to leave home to attend school. He may have had a minor illness or some slight difficulty with a teacher or classmate. The family may have moved, and a school transfer was involved. An illness may have occurred in a member of the family, often the mother. Or circumstances may have required a parent's absence from home for a few days.

The majority of children who have this condition are in the lower grades, with ages ranging from five to nine years. In older children, school phobia may indicate more complicated problems and in adolescents may be part of a more serious mental illness.

Causes for the refusal to attend school may be varied. Most often it has to do with a fear of separation from home, usually connected with feelings about being away from Mother. Many parents of these children have a history of separation from an important person in their own childhood. These parents may find it very difficult to provide the type of firm support that will enable their child to cope with, and master, the feelings about separation.

Another element frequently involved in these children is the handling of their hostile impulses. All youngsters will at some time experience a feeling of rage directed against their parents. The anger can occur over important or trivial matters. Children may momentarily wish that something bad happen to their parents.

What happens next will depend on the existing pattern within a particular family for dealing with angry feelings. Parents may accept hostility as a common feeling that is experienced and can be expressed. Of course, harmful actions that might result from this anger should be controlled. If parents do not have this attitude, a child may feel very guilty for having such an "evil thought." He may suppress it. In its place may come a fear that something will happen to his parent. He may then have to remain physically close to his mother and father because they need to be protected, and his presence, in some magical way, will protect them.

It is generally agreed that these children should be returned to school as quickly as possible. The longer they remain out of school, the more difficult the task of getting them back.

When a child exhibits this refusal to go to school, many approaches are of no avail. These might include bribery, cajoling, threatening, and physical punishment.

What should parents do when confronted with a child's refusal to go to school? If symptoms (such as headache, abdominal pain, or vomiting) are present, the child should be examined by a physician to rule out physical illness. After making sure that there is no disease, the parent can investigate the school or classroom to determine if there is any real difficulty that would justify refusal to attend. When such exists, a change should be suggested. Usually this will not be the case, and changes of teacher or classroom will not help the child.

Parents should understand that the fear of school is rarely due to realistic considerations. It is important to make concerted efforts to have the child return to school as soon as possible. Parents of such a child often have unresolved problems themselves about separation. They find it very difficult to be firm when the youngster cries and shows varying degrees of panicky feeling when he must return to school.

A significant element in the procedure will be the understanding and cooperation of school personnel. They need to be told that it is not the school itself that the child fears, and that it is essential for him to return as soon as possible.

Some children can be returned directly to their classroom, while others may have to go back in stages, perhaps spending some time in the principal's, or counselor's, office with attempts later to return to class. Occasionally the mother's presence in the school may be helpful, providing the child does not become completely dependent on her being there.

In some instances it may be necessary for the teacher to receive the child from the parent and physically keep him in the classroom until separation from the parent has been effected. Such handling often works well with a child in the first few grades. The teacher needs to know that this pupil is not hurt by this experience, and in fact that she may be helping him.

Once the necessary arrangements have been made with the school, the child should be told that he must go back to school. We can tell him we know that he will be frightened, but nothing will happen to him or members of his family while he is in school. Since he must go back, it would be better for him to go, if possible, without tears and fighting to save himself embarrassment. If he has been absent for any length of time, a face-saving excuse can be given to him to be used when schoolmates question him. For example, he could say that he had not been feeling well, but now the doctor says he can come back to school.

When a child is "forced" to go to school, he may become very angry. He may tell his parents, "You hate me or you wouldn't do this to me." Or he may say that he hates them. In fact, parents and teachers should be aware that the child may have an openly hostile reaction.

It can be very helpful to a child if his anger does not "win the day," and if the parent, or teacher, kindly and firmly tells him that he has a right to feel angry, that the feelings of anger will not hurt him or anybody else, and that he must go to school and stay in school. With some children the ventilation of some of their hostility at a time like this can have a beneficial effect on their emotional development, if the adults involved take it in stride.

No matter what the underlying cause may be, when a child remains out of school he loses opportunities for associating with his peers. He loses the opportunity to master the situation and to progress in his education, and there is a decrease in his self-esteem.

Many younger children can be returned to school quickly. After a weekend at home or a vacation, the difficulty may recur, and parents should be firm on the day school begins again.

If a child cannot be returned to school, professional help should be obtained from a psychiatrist or mental health clinic. Psychiatric consultation is particularly indicated in the case of adolescents who develop a fear of school.

CHAPTER IV

Handicapped Children

The Parent's Feelings

"When I first heard that my baby had been born without an arm, I had an awful thought. I wished he had died at birth. At that moment I felt it would have been better if that had happened."

IF YOU are the parent of a child who has a severe physical or mental handicap and you have sometimes wished that the child had died, if you have felt guilt believing you were in some way responsible for your child's defect, if you have felt ashamed and horrified for not giving birth to a completely healthy infant, if you have felt unsure of your ability to be a good parent to a severely handicapped child, if you have worried excessively about what will happen to your child, or if you have had extreme anger because of what has occurred and have wondered, "Why did it have to happen to us?"—then you have shared the experiences of most parents of offspring with birth defects.

Handicapped children present special problems for parents. In order to give a child the help he will need, parents must first deal with their own feelings about the disability.

Sometimes the upsetting situation is apparent immediately, at birth. We usually look forward to the coming of a child, the anticipation of a happy occasion. Nevertheless, there are instances when an infant is born with an obvious defect, such as a missing arm or leg.

This of course is disturbing to everyone. The doctor, upset by the development, may not tell the mother much about the new baby, and she senses something is wrong. A doctor may not permit the mother to see the infant, and she will imagine that the baby is more deformed than is the case. With some defects, in an effort to be helpful a doctor may say, "We'll be able to help you with all these problems later." This may leave the parents with certain unfulfillable hopes. Most parents are somewhat relieved when they actually see their baby because the idea of the defect is worse for them than the actual sight.

Anyone who is associated with the parents of children with birth defects should realize that these parents should have the right to grieve. Such parents almost *need* to express death wishes toward the child; leaving these thoughts unexpressed may lead to feelings of guilt or rejection which will interfere with healthy parent-child relationships.

Parents must work out their feelings of guilt. Too often they blame themselves for actions or wishes that they consider to be a causative factor for their youngster's handicap. They may need to be told that the fact that they considered abortion during the pregnancy could have no effect on the developing embryo. Even if a mother had taken a dangerous drug, such as Thalidomide, she did not take it knowing that this would have a bad effect on the fetus.

Parents need the opportunity to give vent to feelings of anger about what fate has dealt them and their child. They need to know that, while all of us may have doubts about our adequacy as parents, these concerns will be much greater if we have a handicapped child.

Some conditions are not obvious at birth; in these cases, parents may handle their feelings in different ways. The parents of a retarded child, for example, may deny the reality of the retardation. While the child's slowness is obvious to almost everyone, the parent may pick on one isolated activity that seems close to normal and insist that this indicates there is no intellectual deficit. Unfortunately, attitudes of denial interfere with efforts that might help the child.

In some cases, a parent may unjustifiably blame others for the child's condition and remain very bitter about it. The projecting of blame in this manner may also hinder legitimate attempts to help the youngster.

Parents of a handicapped child will not only have fears

about his future, but they may be afraid to have other children. These parents would benefit greatly from genetic counseling. They need to find out if there are any realistic bases for their apprehension in relation to having additional children.

As parents of handicapped children, we should not be ashamed of our feelings. We can be aware that we and our youngster will have difficulties to face. We may all feel some sensitivity about our child's appearance. We should not think badly of ourselves if, for example, we were uncomfortable about handling our amputee child at first.

I have seen the parents of severely handicapped children accept them, love them, and become very proud of them. I am amazed at how these children learn to cope, and together with their parents, I respect them for this.

The Child's Feelings

Timmy, an amputee, was playing in front of his house. A new boy in the neighborhood came over, stared at him, and said, "What happened to your leg? Did they cut it off because you were bad?"

THERE IS always the possibility that children with obvious handicaps will be exposed to experiences similar to this episode. People will stare at them. In fact, most of us find it difficult not to stare at an amputee or at anyone who is noticeably different.

A child's success in accepting his handicap and compensating for it will be determined mainly by the attitudes of his parents. The child presents special child-rearing problems. The parents, because of feelings of guilt or out of sympathy for the child's plight, may be reluctant to set limits for this youngster in the same way they would for a completely healthy offspring. Still, it is important to treat the child as much like a normal child as possible, and this includes discipline when necessary.

Parents need to understand and accept the limitations imposed by the particular handicap. They should learn from the physician, psychologist, occupational therapist, and physical therapist what the child's capabilities are. With this information in hand, they should expect the child to do what he is capable of doing, and should not try to make things too easy for him because of his disability.

The child with a handicap will want to know why he is different. The younger preschool child should be told, "because you were born this way." Too often a child is told, "God made you this way." Do not tell this to a child. If he is given this as an explanation for his condition, he will wonder why God picked on him. He may feel he has been punished for something. The handicapped child should be told that the disability he has is not due to anything he has said, thought, or done.

The child can be told that people may stare at him and make comments about his handicap. If he tells us he has heard a statement similar to the one the boy in our example made to Timmy, we should tell him that many people do not understand about handicaps and they may say things that are not right. He may hear some adult say, "Oh, you poor boy, to have that awful thing happen to you," or, "I feel so sorry for you, you poor child." We should tell the youngster that we are not sorry for him because, even though he has a handicap, he is as good a person as anyone else.

We should tell the child that if other children or adults ask what happened to him, he can simply say he was born this way. If his condition resulted from an illness or injury, he can answer honestly that he had an accident or sickness.

Our goal with a handicapped child must be to make him feel that he is a person of worth, no matter what his problem.

It is important to do this throughout his early years so that by his adolescence he will have sufficient self-esteem to cope with his relationships to others.

A child should be permitted to express his anger at what has happened to him. He can be told that he is not the only person to whom this has happened and other people in his situation would feel angry too. We ourselves would feel angry if we had this handicap. But, we must encourage him to attempt new things and let him know it is no disgrace to fail at something that is difficult for him. We should tell him we expect him to do the best he can.

We can keep in mind that a handicapped child may have an increased need to be dependent on us, but we should allow and encourage acts of independence. We should avoid letting the handicap itself become the basis for a way of life. A child with a marked handicap will experience more anxiety than an ordinary child when he has to face new experiences. He needs more of our support and encouragement. Where there is a possibility of his accomplishing something successfully, we should get him to try rather than help him to avoid the experience.

Children with handicaps often amaze us with their ability to compensate for their defects. If we respect them and their accomplishments, they will gain more respect for themselves.

When a handicapped child becomes an adolescent, he may want much more of an explanation about why he is different. If there is more definite information available than what he previously was told, he should be given truthful answers. He may want to know if he should marry and whether he should have children.

If his condition is due to a birth injury, or to the fact that his mother had German measles or harmful medication during pregnancy, he can be assured that this will not affect his future offspring. If a condition is hereditary, the teen-ager can be told that there are specialists who do genetic counseling with whom he will be able to discuss things and have some of his questions answered. These doctors will be able to tell him what percentage chance there could be of his offspring developing a similar condition. This type of information can be helpful to any individual in making decisions about marriage and subsequently about having children or adopting them.

The Sibling's Feelings

Stanley was a two-year-old who had been born without a right foot. His five-year-old sister, Linda, came to her mother and said, "I wish they would take my foot off so I could be like him."

"You mustn't say things like that, Linda," her mother told her.

THE SIBLINGS of a child who is handicapped need understanding and support. They too will have a variety of feelings to cope with.

Often, parents must devote an inordinate amount of time to the handicapped child. The other children, especially those of preschool age, will have dependency needs of their own. They may become very angry because of the feeling that they are being neglected. They may actually have the wish, as Linda did, to be defective in some way so that they can get more attention.

When a child expresses anger, directly or indirectly, about this situation, she should not be shamed or made to feel guilty. She can be told that we understand how she would be upset because her brother needs all the extra attention and she may feel we do not care enough about her. We should assure her that we love her as much as we do her brother or any other child.

In a family where a baby is born with an obvious defect, it is important, for the sake of this handicapped child, that the parents provide the opportunity in the home for open discussion of the handicap. This should begin with the father telling the siblings about it before the mother and infant return from the hospital.

The other children in the family may have various emotional reactions to this information. We all know that normally many siblings wish their mother was not having another baby, or at least they have very mixed feelings about it. When the new infant is born with a disability, his brothers and sisters may feel that their hostile wishes caused the baby's defect. The father should tell them we do not know why the baby was born with an abnormality, but we are sure that no thoughts or wishes of his siblings had anything to do with the infant's troubles.

If there are children of eighteen months to four years of age in the family, the normally present fear of bodily hurt may be increased when they hear or see that part of the baby's body is missing. They may express the fear directly, or they may begin to have bad dreams or fears of various objects or animals. They should be told that the baby was born this way, and that nothing like this will happen to them.

When the healthy children are older and attending school, they may feel embarrassed about the handicapped sibling and may express this to their parents. Sometimes they will feel this way, but be reluctant to say so for fear of hurting their parents' feelings. We need to be aware of this possibility.

The handicap involved may be a physical deformity, mental retardation, or the effect of brain damage. Regardless of the type of disability, the children should be told that it is not wrong to feel sensitive about the appearance or behavior of their handicapped sibling. We can tell them that it is not their fault or the affected child's fault that he is the way he is. We can say that it is probably true that the family's life would be easier in many ways if the one member did not have his disability. However, we should also tell them that there are positive aspects to overcoming adversity, and they too can gain something by knowing they are contributing to helping the sibling cope with his difficulties.

We should avoid comparing the behavior of our healthy offspring with the handicapped one. For example, we should not shame a child about particular actions by saying, "Look, your brother doesn't do that and he's got more problems than you." In fact, we should not compare two healthy children in this way. We can tell a child that we disapprove of his behavior without comparing him to a sister or brother.

Youngsters quickly learn that they can get a sibling in trouble by doing something when the parent is not watching and then yelling when retaliation occurs. When a handicapped child is involved, the parent may be too quick to blame the healthy one. If the child objects to this, the parent may say, "Well, it doesn't matter who started it, you know he has problems." Such handling is unwise; it is unfair to the healthy child, and unhealthy for the afflicted one. He has special needs in terms of his care, but he should not have this type of special privilege when it comes to his relationship to siblings. In the interest of all the children in a family, especially the handicapped one, the atmosphere in the home should be one in which all members of the family can live with the disability and the problems it produces.

School Problems

"I will not have that child with the hook in my school," said the principal. *"He will frighten many children and cause a disturbance in the school."*

THE FIFTH-GRADE student involved in this episode had previously been attending a special school for handicapped children.

He was a very attractive boy who had been born without an arm. He used a prosthetic device ("hook") which he handled very well. He could do most of the things he was required to do.

Unless a disability is very severe, our aim should be to have the child take his place in as normal a setting as possible. When it was decided to send this student to his neighborhood public school, the principal reacted in a very unfortunate manner.

The child's parents were tremendously upset; they did not know what to do. When they insisted that their son had a right to attend the school, the principal said that the child would have to go before the children and tell them about his condition so that they would not be frightened.

Fortunately, the parents did not go along with this ill-advised plan. They shared their concerns with a social worker who had worked with them and the child in an amputee clinic. The parents were assured that the principal's attitude was an unhealthy one. If anyone should not have been in that school, it was the principal rather than the child.

It would have been cruel to make this youngster feel he was so abnormal that he had to reassure the other students. Such a child needs to be told by words and actions that he is as worthwhile as any other youngster, and there should be no implication he is so horrible that the other pupils will be frightened of him.

This principal was advised not to subject the boy to the type of handling she had suggested. She was also told that, if any of the children became seriously disturbed by the sight of the boy's amputation and hook, it probably indicated that they needed help with their feelings. When other children become fearful on seeing a handicapped child, we should tell them that the affected youngster was born this way, and that this is not going to happen to them.

Before a handicapped child is ready to go to school, the parents should meet with the principal and teacher to discuss his condition, and let the school know what he is capable of doing and what he may not be able to do. Fortunately, most school personnel are cooperative, although they may have their own limitations when it comes to dealing with handicapped students. If necessary, the parents may request that a doctor or social worker talk to them and advise them. The child's disability may prevent him from doing certain things. But aside from this, the school should have the same expectations of him as they do of the other students.

Should Retarded Children Be Kept at Home?

"Your baby has all the characteristics of Mongolism," the doctor said.
"What does this mean?" inquired Mr. Brown.
"He will definitely be retarded and I think you should arrange to put him in an institution as soon as possible."

THE QUESTION of institutionalization for a retarded child is a complicated one. There are those who feel it is best to put an infant in an institution as soon as possible. The thinking behind this view is that it becomes increasingly difficult for the parents to give the child up after he has lived in the home. While this may be true, there are good reasons for not following this course.

It is difficult in many cases to predict the outcome by observing an infant during the first few months of life. At times babies surprise us by the gains they make after an initial period of slow development. Some children show a very uneven type of functioning later. They may be able in certain areas, such as verbal abilities, but lack capacity where physical dexterity is necessary. These youngsters can compensate for many of their deficiencies. It would be a mistake to try to evaluate at an early age just how retarded they are.

As the child grows and develops, the degree of retardation will become more apparent. Some individuals will have to be cared for all their lives. Others will be capable of at least caring for their own needs and perhaps doing simple work in a sheltered workshop. Still others can be educated sufficiently so they can hold down an uncomplicated job. The fact that the outcome is so hard to predict argues for keeping a young child at home instead of putting him into an institution.

Even if a baby is definitely retarded, there is a good reason for having him remain with his parents at least through the first five or six years of his life. Hopefully, the parents will be able to work out their own feelings of guilt, anger, shame, disappointment, and of failure at having had a defective child. And, by being with them, the child will gain something that is very necessary for him.

For the overriding reason for living with the family is that the child will learn what it is like to be close to, and relate to, others. By our care, love, and discipline we will be telling him that he is worthwhile to us. Even if he has to go to an institution later on, the experience at home will help him to get along better with others in the institution.

Every infant should experience what it is like to be close to another human being. The mother is the one to whom the baby first relates; she feeds him, keeps him dry and comfortable, cuddles him, and in general loves him. This is as important for the retarded infant as for anyone else.

Along with their concern for the retarded child, parents should be attentive to the needs of their normal children. The siblings should be given an explanation of the condition and limitations of the affected child. The retarded child's behavior may at times anger his brothers and sisters. We should understand they have a right to be angry and we should give them permission for their feelings. They should be told, however, that they should not tease their sibling about his condition.

Once the degree of retardation becomes evident, each retarded child must be considered on an individual basis. Besides infancy there are two other peak periods when the question of institutionalization will arise. One is at school-entry age; here the difficulty of continuing to care for the child at home may become apparent. The other is during adolescence when the upsurge in sexual and aggressive impulses may create problems for the retarded child who may have very poor judgment. It may be necessary to put him in a protected environment to prevent his getting into serious difficulty.

In many instances we may have to weigh the welfare of the retarded youngster against the welfare of the family's other children. It is a most difficult decision for parents to make. It is well to remember that the older retarded child has had the benefit of being at home during his developmental years. Later he may be as well off in an institution, where he will have the companionship of others with similar ability. As hard as it is for parents to separate themselves from their child, they may have to do it for the sake of the child and the siblings.

When an individual will require care for the rest of his life, the parents should make plans that will not place the burden on the siblings. It is unfair to sacrifice the welfare and future of the healthy children.

Minimal Brain Dysfunction and Hyperactivity

David's father was describing his four-year-old son's behavior to the pediatrician. "We don't know what to do about that boy. He's clumsy. We can't tell if he's right-handed or left-handed. He won't sit still for a minute and he can't keep his attention on anything. He's got to touch everything he sees. Even though I've spanked him a lot, he doesn't under-

stand the word 'No.' I swear, Doctor, he's like a high-powered car with a motor running all the time and no brakes."

IT HAS been estimated that at least three out of every one hundred elementary school children can be described as hyperactive and distractible. These children have also been called "hyperkinetic." More boys than girls seem to have this increase in activity. A large number of such youngsters will also have other characteristics, some of which were exhibited by David.

Many names have been given to the collection of symptoms that these children show. Probably the term most commonly heard nowadays is "minimal brain dysfunction." This name suggests that particular areas of the child's brain are not working properly. Some of these children have a history of a difficult birth which may have resulted in mild brain damage. Others have a family history which indicates that their parents, or other relatives, had similar problems in their childhood. But in many youngsters, there is no apparent definite cause for the problem.

The child with minimal brain dysfunction may have a few or many of the following symptoms: he may be overactive; he may have a short attention span and be very distractible; he may have trouble controlling his impulses and a low tolerance for frustration; he may have poor coordination and difficulty learning to do things such as riding a tricycle; his speech may be delayed or there may be indistinct speech; he may be slow in picking out his handedness; he may have mild visual problems or some degree of hearing impairment; he may have trouble learning to read or a specific learning disability for arithmetic.

Because of his difficulty in controlling himself, a hyperactive child gets into a great deal of trouble and is frequently punished. His parents are often as perplexed as were David's parents. Unless a physician informs them that their child cannot control most of his behavior, they may feel he is just being naughty. Grandparents, other relatives, and friends usually blame the parents' handling for the child's actions and are ready with simple advice for remedying the situation, perhaps saying, "All that boy needs is a good whipping." But beatings do no good.

The child may begin to look upon himself as bad. One boy said, "I must have a devil in me who makes me do the things I do." It is very likely that many of these children will grow up with very little self-esteem.

As far as intelligence is concerned, these youngsters may be retarded or dull-normal or extremely bright. When they are given intelligence tests, their IQ scores may be relatively meaningless; there are often marked differences in their performance on various parts of the test.

It is important for parents to be aware of the possibility that a child may have minimal brain dysfunction. These children are not bad. They cannot control themselves and will need help in doing so.

If a parent suspects that her preschool offspring fits the picture of a hyperactive child, she should discuss this with her physician. Certain specialized examinations may be indicated, such as a neurological examination, psychological testing, and speech, hearing, and vision evaluations. Medication can be very helpful and may be prescribed by the physician.

Much controversy has arisen over the use of drugs to control hyperactivity and distractibility in children. If a hyperactive child is given a sedative drug, such as phenobarbital, his behavior will usually get worse. Surprisingly, a good percentage of these youngsters can be helped by giving them stimulant drugs. These drugs do not pep up the hyperactive child as they would other people. Rather, the medication decreases purposeless activity and helps the child concentrate on his work and focus his attention better. The drugs are not a cure-all, but if they help a child control himself, he will benefit from the better relationships he can have with others, and from his success in school.

In addition to medication, these children are more in need of firm and consistent limits than is the average child. Sometimes we need to watch out that they are not overstimulated by their environment. For example, a hyperactive distractible child may be able to play well with one other youngster, but at a birthday party or other large gathering, he may be almost uncontrollable.

If a child is markedly hyperactive and has trouble controlling himself, he should be told that he is not a bad boy. He can be told that he was born more active than some other children and that this will improve as he gets older. Many children think they are the only ones with this problem, and they should be told that quite a few youngsters have the same difficulties. If he complains that his parents are always stopping him from doing things he wants to do, they should explain that it is hard for him to stop himself so they have to help him by stopping him.

Some pre-teen children balk at taking their medication even though it helps them. One boy would not take medicine when he was angry with his parents. He knew it calmed him down, but he wanted to misbehave because of his anger. We should explain to a hyperactive child that having to take medicine does not mean he is not a good person. The medicine is to help him so that he can pay attention better and learn more.

Many of these children require special education classes and methods. Unfortunately, these are often unavailable. Certain things can be done to help such a child in a regular classroom. Of prime importance, the teacher should be made aware that he has a special problem. If drugs are helpful these should be prescribed. The child should be given a seat in the classroom where there are the least number of distractions.

Quite a few children with minimal brain dysfunction can compensate for much of their handicap, especially if the condition is recognized before the start of school or in the lower grades. If parents and teachers understand what is wrong with a child, they will not put undue pressure on him to accomplish what he is unable to do. Sometimes just giving him additional time to complete his work will be a help. He may need special instruction to overcome some of his deficiencies.

By the time most of these children are adolescents, the hyperactivity tends to decrease. Our aim should be to get them to this point feeling that they are worthwhile people. These youngsters will need more parental support and encouragement than other children do. We should try to note what particular abilities and interests they have and help them in developing these.

The Mildly Handicapped Child

"Mom," said Johnny, "I don't like it when the kids keep calling me the 'Jolly Green Giant.' I wish I wasn't so tall."

THERE ARE many children who we might consider as mildly handicapped. They can experience a good bit of discomfort because of their condition.

Youngsters who are the shortest or tallest, or fattest or skinniest in the class become concerned about themselves. Often the other students make comments about them, and give them nicknames.

Some youngsters are very awkward. This can be quite uncomfortable, especially for boys, in a culture where athletic ability is valued.

Other children have speech problems and are unable to say certain letters and words properly. They may be teased about this and called "dumb" because of their speech difficulties. If they become upset at the teasing, they are often teased more.

As with any handicapped child, we have to help the mildly handicapped one maintain his self-esteem. It is extremely important to give him the feeling that his parents like him the way he is. We should avoid frequent references to height and weight and avoid comparing him to friends and siblings.

The child who is very tall or very short for his age should be assured that such variations are normal and there is nothing physically wrong with him. If he complains about being teased we should listen to him and not make fun of him by pooh-poohing his concerns. We can tell him that he knows we think he is fine the way he is, and the children who tease others may also be very unsure of themselves. If we have tall or short friends whom our child knows, we can tell him that they had to put up with the same sort of annoyance in their school days.

With any mildly handicapped children we should not tell them they have no right to be annoyed because of their differences. The awkward child will be unhappy about his clumsiness. There is probably little we can tell him directly that will be of great comfort. One boy, now a college student, once had a definite problem with awkwardness but was still able to maintain a large measure of self-esteem. He was recently asked what he could have been told that would have helped with his feelings about the lack of dexterity. He answered, "The only thing that could have helped me would have been if someone had told me that I'd wake up tomorrow and be a good athlete."

He was actually helped by being permitted to verbalize his unhappiness about his lack of athletic ability. He was told by his parents that, while they understood his feelings, it was not his fault or theirs that he was born this way, and it was something that could not change. He was encouraged to do the best he could, and his father practiced with him when the boy asked. He knew from their attitude that they liked him and valued him for the person he was.

We can rarely do much about a child's height. We may

be able to help children with their coordination by enrolling them in special physical education programs. We can secure speech therapy for the youngster with a speech problem. But we can help every child by telling him in words and actions that we want him, that we think he is a fine person, and that we are satisfied with him as he is.

CHAPTER V

Death

Explaining Death and Burial

"I flew up here on an airplane from North Carolina," the boy told the doctor, "and I looked on every cloud, but I didn't see her."

"Whom were you looking for?" asked the doctor.

"My mother," answered the boy. "When she died, they told me she had gone up in the sky, and I looked for her on every cloud, but she wasn't there. I was disappointed."

THIS LITTLE boy actually believed that he would find his mother on a cloud in the sky. And from what he had been told about his mother's death, this was a reasonable expectation. He had not attended the funeral, but had been kept busy by well-meaning relatives who wanted to spare him as much unhappiness as possible.

Death is an ever-present fact of life. It is a part of the natural order of things—to be born, to live, and to die. But it is a subject that makes most of us uncomfortable. We would prefer not to think about it. Unless a person suffers from a severe depression, he does not want to contemplate his no longer "being."

Our culture attempts to deny the reality of death. The deceased person is cosmetically made to appear as he did in life. We find it difficult to accept the fact of death, and even more difficult to tell a child about death. This is especially true of the death of someone with whom the child has had a close, ongoing relationship.

The age of the child affects his concept of death. To a young child, death is not an irreversible process. He may think that a person dies and then returns. This tendency to think of death as something that is not final may be reinforced by what a child is told. For example, if someone says "Grandpa has gone to sleep and won't get up anymore," or "He passed away," or "Your daddy has gone on a long trip but he's never coming back," the child may be confused but still have the expectation that he will see the dead person again.

It is important to be direct and truthful with children in discussing a death in the family or the death of a close friend. When children are not given factual information they supply their own explanation about events, and often the things they imagine are more bizarre than the truth. Frequently, these fantasies are very frightening to them.

Obviously, the youngster who searched for his mother on every cloud should have been treated differently. He should have been told that his mother had died and that her body had been buried in the ground, and that it would remain in the ground. He could have been told that death means we will never see her again, but we can always remember and love her and know that she loved us.

If he had any questions about her illness, an explanation should have been offered to him in words appropriate to his age. One should be aware that a child, upon hearing that someone has died of sickness, may be afraid that any illness will then be extremely dangerous to him. The child should have been told that he would not catch his mother's disease, and that while many people become ill, most people recover from their illness, especially young people.

Religious beliefs that are strongly held can be a great source of comfort at a time of bereavement. If a parent believes in a life after death and wants his children to share his belief, he should tell the child that the body of a dead person remains in the ground while the soul, or spirit, ascends to heaven.

If a family does not believe in a life after death, the child could be told that one does not know what happens to a person after death, but the important thing is how one lives his life.

Even though we are truthful and give a child factual information about death and burial, the child may still deny the reality of what has happened. He may still say "Mommy will be coming home soon." The adults about him should listen to the child. They should, without undue prodding, attempt to learn from the child's words and actions what misconceptions he may have about death.

Recently, a five-year-old boy whose sister had been killed told me that his sister was buried in a coffin. He had been told by a cousin that, while the girl was dead and buried, she could still hear in the coffin. He also believed that a person could get out of a coffin; he had seen a man on television do so as an introduction to a horror movie. The boy was greatly relieved to learn that these ideas were absolutely untrue.

If mistaken ideas are held by the child, he should not be laughed at or made to feel foolish. Patient attempts should be made to correct his erroneous thoughts or feelings about what has occurred.

Funerals

"May I go to the funeral?"
"No, I think you'd better not go," said the mother. Why should the child too be exposed to the unhappiness?

MANY PARENTS mistakenly believe that they should, or could, protect their children from unhappiness. Even if it were possible to do so, it would not be a good idea. In the same way that a child must learn to tolerate frustration by experiencing frustration in small doses, so must he learn that unhappiness exists in life, and that he will have to face unhappy events in his daily life.

A person who has been shielded from having to deal with tragedy of any kind will have difficulty coping when the inevitable misfortune befalls him. The child learns how to deal with adversity from the attitudes of the significant people to whom he feels close; and being with them during periods of unhappiness is part of this learning experience.

When a parent or close relative dies, the question is often asked, "Should the children attend the funeral?" The answer is that the child, if he is old enough to understand what is taking place, should certainly be offered the opportunity to take part in this ceremony marking the end of the life of a person who is meaningful to him. Young children, perhaps six years and under, who may not be able to control their behavior well enough, should not be permitted to attend the funeral. However, one should honestly try to answer any questions the child has about the funeral in words that he can understand.

Older children can be encouraged to attend the funeral. One should not be concerned because the child will see upset and grieving people at the funeral. The child will learn that it is normal to have these feelings at a time like this. Attending the funeral will reinforce in the child's consciousness the reality of what has occurred, and aid in keeping him from developing unrealistic ideas about death.

Parents should, however, be aware of the fact that their mixed feelings about the child's attendance at the funeral may be communicated in the way they offer the invitation. A parent who is concerned with protecting the child from unhappiness may say, "You don't want to go to the funeral, do you?" This parent may feel that he has permitted the child to go, but the child may get the actual message: the parent is uncomfortable about his attendance.

The child should be made to feel that he has a right to attend the funeral. Some adults remember how angry they were for many, many years because during their childhood one of their parents died and they were denied the privilege of going to the funeral. Sometimes the poor handling is made worse by sending a child off to the movies or distracting him in other ways, to make it seem as if the tragedy has not really happened.

If a child objects strenuously to going to the funeral, he should not be forced to go, and he should not be made to feel guilty about not attending. As with the younger child, any questions that he has before or after the funeral should be answered honestly. Later, the child can be encouraged to visit the cemetery accompanied by an adult whom he trusts.

The child who is denied the opportunity of being a participant in times of sadness is also denied the healing effect of grief.

Permitting Grief

William had been crying. His father had died and he was feeling miserable. His uncle, seeing him sob, told him, "Now, now there, fella, big men don't cry."

SOMEHOW, THE idea persists in our culture that it is unmanly to have feelings of tenderness or openly to exhibit one's emotions, even on those occasions when one would naturally feel like crying and should be permitted to do so.

Children, especially males, are often told that they must be brave, "Keep a stiff upper lip," and not give vent to their emotions by crying. Many a boy has felt like crying, and would have benefited by the release of his tension in this way, but has kept himself from tears because this would not be consistent with "being a man."

Courage should not be equated with the absence of feelings of tenderness and sympathy. It should not be equated with the withholding of open expression of sadness when events occur that cause great unhappiness.

When children cry we should try to understand, if possible, what it is that they are crying about. At times it may be impossible for us to fathom what is behind the tears. At other times the cause may be clear; for example, when they've had a great disappointment or suffered a loss of some kind.

We all have known of a child whose pet has died or been killed. The child's parents become concerned as to how their offspring will react to this news. Frequently a parent with good, but misguided, intentions will seek to replace the pet before the child comes home so that the youngster may not even know that his hamster or goldfish has died. Where the child cannot be fooled in this manner, he may be told that his dog ran away, rather than that the animal died.

It would be better to be truthful with the child and permit him to experience whatever feelings of sadness and grief that occur. We should do some thinking about what we say to children. Perhaps we should find other ways of telling children what is going to happen to their pet than to say, "We're taking Rover to the vet's to be put to sleep." Hearing such a statement could produce a fear in the child of his own going to sleep at night. It makes more sense to tell the child that a sick or infirm animal is so uncomfortable we are taking it to the veterinarian so that it can die comfortably.

In a hospital where I worked, a child who died was literally spirited away in the night because some members of the staff were concerned about how they could deal with the other young patients' feelings if they found out about the death. The children were told that the dead child had been transferred during the night, but they could not find out where he had been sent, so most of them really did not believe this anyway. Sooner or later they found out from an older child that the child had died. These children would naturally wonder why they were not told the truth, and they would worry more about their own dying and disappearing in the way that their hospital mate had disappeared.

The situation improved in this hospital when the staff began to understand some of these things, and on the relatively rare occasions that a death occurred on the children's ward, the other patients were told. An attempt was always made to find out from the other children how they felt about the child's death, and what questions and concerns they themselves had. Many children were afraid that they would die. They were assured that, while it was true that children sometimes die, they were not going to die because of the illness or physical condition that made it necessary for them to come into the hospital; and that, like most people, they would probably live to an old age. They were also told that it was all right to be sad about losing a friend and, if they felt like crying, that it was all right to cry.

When a parent or close relative dies, it is normal and desirable to grieve over them. Individuals who do not permit themselves to grieve over the loss of a dear one have in a sense left a job undone; later, they may develop symptoms of depression or unjustified guilt feelings because of these unresolved emotions.

Children should not only be permitted to show their grief but also encouraged to do so. They should be told that it is perfectly normal to feel sad and to cry when something very unhappy occurs. This is one of the reasons why we should not try to stop children from attending a funeral if they want to go. It will do them no harm if they see their friends and relatives saddened and crying. Children should be permitted to take part in the mourning process and to learn that it is not cowardly or unmanly to cry when an occasion justifies the shedding of tears.

Sometimes children are concerned about not talking about a dead person; they are afraid of precipitating evidence of sadness or tears in their parents. Recently, a teen-age girl died. Her five-year-old brother did not talk much about it because he thought that, if he did, his mother would become sad and tearful. When his mother became aware of this, she told him that it was all right to talk about his sister, even if Mother seemed sad. Mother missed her and the thought did make her unhappy, but he was assured that there was nothing wrong with feeling unhappiness at a time like this, and his talking about what happened to his sister was not doing his mother any harm. In fact, she was relieved that they could be at ease in *sharing* their grief—each expressing it in his own way.

Fear of Abandonment

"Daddy died," said Susan. "Mommy, are you going to die too and leave me alone? Who will take care of me?"

ONE OF the basic needs of a child is that of dependency. The newborn infant is totally dependent for his survival on someone other than himself. He needs to be fed, to be kept warm and dry, to be cuddled and loved and talked to so that he develops a feeling of what it is like to be close to another human being.

During the latter part of his first year of life, the infant develops the physical capacity to crawl away from his mother. He also begins to experience an uncomfortable feeling which results from his being separated from this person on whom he has come to depend and who protects him. If his mother is only out of his sight, he will cry. This sensation of discomfort experienced by the baby is called "separation anxiety." It is a feeling that can be rekindled by various circumstances in a person's life; in fact, we all must cope with it from time to time.

From the time that a baby crawls away from his mother and experiences separation anxiety, he begins working out the interrelationship between his need to be dependent and his natural drive to become independent. In this process he very much requires the help of good parents who will meet his dependency needs and also, at the proper times, encourage him in his strivings for independence.

If a parent does an adequate job of helping a child progress from a state of being dependent to a state of being able to function independently, the parent should become "dispensable." By this I mean that the young adult should no longer "need" to be with his parent but, presumably, at times would want to be with the parent. In other words, by the time a child becomes an adult he should have resolved most of his conflict between his dependency needs and his drive to achieve independent status. The individual who successfully accomplishes this can be said to be "interdependent," able to both give and take where emotional requirements are involved.

Even after we have reached the point of being able to handle our own needs well, we will still experience a feeling of loss when someone we have loved dies. When a parent dies leaving young children, the offspring experience a feeling of abandonment. "Who will take care of me?" is a very legitimate question. Even if they do not ask it out loud, they are probably thinking about it.

A wife feels abandoned when her husband dies. When her child asks, "Mommy, are you going to die too?" the mother might actually feel, "I wish I could." She herself is frightened about facing life without the support of her husband. It is difficult at a time of bereavement to ask a widow or widower to think of priorities, but it is extremely important to remember the child's vulnerability at such a time.

Children are very concerned about who will take care of them, for being able to depend on someone is a fundamental need of the child. The fear of being abandoned is a very real one. We should attempt to do what we can to calm as much of this fear as possible.

If a child voices concern over whether his remaining parent will die he should be told that, although everyone will die someday, it is likely that the parent will live a long life and that the youngster will no doubt be grown up and have a family of his own by the time his other parent dies.

Sometimes a child will listen to such an explanation and still say, or at least think to himself, "Yes, but what if you don't live that long?" This brings up a matter that is of significance to any of us who have young children. We have all heard of automobile and plane accidents where both parents have been killed simultaneously. It is almost mandatory that we think through the question of whom we would want to care for our children in the event that something happened to us.

Whom would we select? Whose values would we want our children to be exposed to if we were not here? What arrangements would cause the least disruption in the lives of our youngsters if we both died?

It is important for all except very young children to have such information, but especially so for those who already have lost one parent and fear the loss of the surviving parent. Such children should be told who will take care of them in the unlikely situation of the remaining parent dying. This can be very reassuring to the child who must cope with this fear of abandonment.

Where pre-adolescent and adolescent children are involved, they can be given more specific information, such as what financial arrangements have been made for their future and what plans have been considered in planning for their education.

Children's Guilt

"It's my fault she died," sobbed the little girl. *"If I hadn't been angry with Mother and wished she'd go away, she wouldn't have gotten sick and died."*

IN MOMENTS of anger many children have wished that their parents were dead. Some youngsters will say openly, "I hate you. I wish you were dead." Others will have such a thought but dare not utter it.

Certainly every child, at one time or another, harbors

angry feelings toward his parents, even though he loves them most of the time. But children must depend on their mother and father for support of various kinds, and the possibility of something happening to their parents is a frightening prospect. A child often feels very guilty when he entertains hostile wishes toward his parents.

The fact that he in some way can be responsible for illness befalling his parents can be reinforced by what they have said to him. Are there many parents who have not at some time said "You're giving me a headache" or "You're making me sick with all that noise" or "You're driving me nuts"?

Children should be told during their early years that it is permissible to have angry feelings. Everyone has such emotions and each of us must find acceptable ways to handle our anger. It is all right to feel as if you would like to shoot someone, but it would be wrong actually to shoot him. In the course of his development the youngster should learn that he can be angry with his mother and father, and that they can be angry with him, even though they all basically love one another.

Nevertheless, with the death of a parent the young child frequently suffers guilt because of the momentary hostile wishes he has had toward his parent. The child remembers the angry thoughts and is convinced that, in some magical way, he caused the illness or accident that took his parent's life.

It is likely that the child will not tell anyone of his feelings of guilt. Added to this is the likelihood that, when a husband or wife dies, the remaining spouse is often too preoccupied with his or her own grief to be paying much attention to the child. Yet, if the surviving parent cannot be attentive to this situation, it is extremely important for other family members or friends to be aware of the fact that a child frequently is troubled by the unreasonable conviction that he in some way has caused his parent to die.

Because the child may feel this way, we should try to correct his mistaken idea and relieve him of unjustified guilty feelings. We might say to the child, "All boys and girls get angry at their parents sometimes and they may even wish that something would happen to their mother or father, even though they really don't mean it to happen. But if something does happen to a mother or father it is not because of what a boy or girl may have thought when he or she was angry. Wishes and thoughts and feelings can't hurt anybody. Even if you wished that they would get hurt and then they did get hurt, it would just be something that happened at the same time, and not because you wished it to happen."

Death of an Abusive Father

"It's just as well he died. His wife and kids will be better off. He was hardly ever home and, when he was there, he was brutal to those kids and beat them unmercifully."

UNFORTUNATELY, THERE are a few parents who behave toward their children in this unbelievably cruel fashion. The parent is undoubtedly mentally ill; still, it is the child who is the recipient of the beatings and who has been subjected to the hard treatment.

All children feel angry toward their parents at times but, usually, they are far more often pleased by their parents' behavior toward them. The good times more than counterbalance the bad times. And the child may also realize that some of the things that make him angry are being done for his own good. Nevertheless, even children with a good relationship with their parents feel guilty for their anger toward them when a parent dies.

But let us consider the case of the child with a brutalizing parent. There is probably little or nothing in the way of good experiences to compensate for the beatings and mistreatment that he suffers at the hand of his father or mother. The child is probably full of fear and rage.

If such a parent dies, the common reaction of people who know the situation will be that the spouse and children are better off without him. And this is true. They will no longer be exposed to the excessive abuse that they previously experienced.

However, we should be aware that children involved in a negative relationship with a parent will probably have much more difficulty with their feelings of guilt than children who have had a relatively good relationship with a deceased parent. The child who has been frequently mistreated may have wished many times that his father was dead. When this happens he may be relieved of one burden, but he may still have to carry an even worse burden of guilt.

We should tell the child that *anyone* who had been treated as badly as he had been would wish to be rid of his tormentor. But the parent's death could not be caused by anyone's wishes. If, in spite of our talking to such a child, he still remains markedly depressed or shows other evidence of disturbed behavior, he may be very much in need of professional help in order to work out his feelings.

The Child's Anger

"Why did Daddy have to die?" asked Jimmy.
"I don't know," said his mother, "it must be God's will."
"I hate God," Jimmy cried.
"That's not a nice thing to say," replied his mother.

IF SOMETHING that we value highly is suddenly taken from us, it makes us angry. We would like to lash out at whoever it is that takes a prized possession away.

When death occurs to someone we love, we experience the loss in a personal way. So often a wife whose husband has died at an early age will say, "Why did he have to be taken from me?" or, "Why did this have to happen to me?" The injustice of the event makes her cry out for an answer. But there are no answers to be given as to why a person dies before his time.

For some people, deep religious faith can be very supportive at a time like this. Others will be angry at "Fate" for the misfortune that has befallen them. Most people at some time during their mourning process will experience anger at the loss they have sustained. It is almost a necessity for them to work out this anger.

The child who loses a parent also feels angry. He may express it as the little boy did who said "I hate God" for taking his father away. In the child's mind, someone had to be responsible, so it was God's fault. No matter what one's religious beliefs, it is important to remember that it is normal for the child to have this anger, and he should not be made to feel guilty about voicing it. Often the child himself may already feel uncomfortable over the fact that he is experiencing so much anger over the loss.

Some children will not express their anger openly. One eight-year-old boy did not seem angry when his mother died. In fact, he talked about her very little and appeared to go about his life at home as if he were not troubled. In school, however, especially during recess periods, he began to fight a lot with his peers, and the teachers became concerned with his combative behavior.

When this situation was explored in a psychiatric interview, it became clear that he was very angry about his mother's death, but he thought that it was wrong to have this angry feeling. So, instead of expressing his feeling directly, he handled it by fighting with his schoolmates.

We should understand that the death of a parent, a relative, or a friend who has been close to a child, will arouse considerable anger in the child. He should be told that, even though the death was nobody's fault, it is all right for him to feel very angry about it, and that most children would feel the same way if it happened in their family.

In the event that a child does not express any anger openly about the death, it would be advisable to offer him the opportunity to do so. For example, one might say, "Most kids would feel pretty mad if their father died. I wonder if you haven't felt that way even though there's nothing we can do to change what's happened." A child may reply affirmatively or negatively to such a statement, but at least he will know that it is not unusual to have angry feelings in such a situation.

Children Should Be Children

"Don't worry, Mother," said her ten-year-old son. "Now that Daddy's gone, I'll be the man of the house and I'll take care of you."

It is touching to hear these concerned and noble sentiments expressed by a youngster whose father has died. A sensitive boy and mindful of his mother's unhappiness, he is trying to console her. She will miss her husband and the support and companionship that he provided for her. If this mother in any way accepts the premise that her son, either in fact or fantasy, should replace her departed spouse, she will be acting unwisely, however, and she will be doing the child a great disservice.

Unfortunately, well-meaning parents and relatives suggest this faulty plan to a child. In an effort to make the child feel better, someone will say to a son, "Now that your dad is gone, you'll have to be the man of the house." A daughter might hear, "Now that your mother is no longer here, you'll have to take care of things for your dad and brothers."

Occasionally a parent will foster such a situation without

stating it directly. One mother took her son to bed with her every night because she was upset and frightened after her husband had been killed in an accident. The boy found sleeping next to his mother pleasurable, but it also made him very uncomfortable for some reason that he did not understand.

When a parent dies, the family members' existence becomes more difficult. Children may have to assume some duties and responsibilities that they did not have before. Still, children should be permitted to be *children* so that they can grow up to be adequate men and women. They should not be put in the position of assuming adult roles for which they are not yet prepared.

When children, by words or actions, suggest to their surviving parent that they will take the role of the departed mother or father, they should be informed clearly and definitely that this cannot and will not be the case. The child should be told, if necessary, that there may have to be more chores and obligations, but the youngster is still the son or daughter in the family, and the remaining parent will be in charge of things. If an older child begins to "boss" his younger siblings, he should be reminded that he is not the parent, and that while he can be concerned for the welfare of his brothers and sisters, it is not his job to order them around.

Following the death of a parent, children need comforting by the other parent. Physical closeness can be of great help, but the parent should be mindful of how it is given. An arm put firmly and lovingly around a shoulder is quite different from the type of hug that a child finds sexually stimulating.

If a youngster says he is frightened to sleep alone, his mother should not take him into her bed, even though she herself is lonely and might welcome the idea of his being there with her. This applies regardless of whether the child is of the same or opposite sex as the parent. The child should be assured that both he and mother will be all right, but he has his own bed and will continue to sleep there. Mother will sleep alone even though Dad is gone.

When a child is awakened by a bad dream and is frightened,

the seemingly easiest thing to do is to take him into your own bed. Then everyone can get needed rest. This is an unwise way to handle such a situation, however, and can lead to habits and patterns of behavior that will make him uncomfortable and be difficult to change later. It is much better to sit on a chair next to a child's bed and give him an opportunity to express his concerns and fears, and to let him know that he is to remain in his own bed.

Disguised Unhappiness

> "I don't know what's wrong with Tommy, Doctor," his mother said. "He wasn't even sad when his father died and that surprised me because he was very close to him. He seems O.K. at home, but his teacher says he's not paying attention in school."

CHILDREN MAY not show openly how they feel about things that disturb them a great deal. Adults, observing a child's behavior, sometimes mistakenly believe that the child has been unaffected by the death of a parent.

Very young children may not comprehend what has occurred. Older children may not want to accept the reality of the incident and might try to deny the actuality of the event. At times the behavior of visitors who come to pay condolence calls to the family will be confusing to a child; in a home where people are supposed to be in mourning, the atmosphere may take on a cocktail-party air.

A youngster sometimes becomes demanding and clings to his mother. Well-meaning relatives, solicitous of the grieving mother's condition, will send the child away saying, "Mother is upset. Don't bother her now," forgetting that the child also is upset.

When a child loses a parent and does not cry or show his grief openly, we should not assume that he is unaffected by the tragedy. We should be observant of his behavior in an effort to determine whether or not he is having problems that are the result of hidden and unresolved feelings.

Has a previously placid and seemingly comfortable child become hyperactive and agitated? Has he developed tics? Is he having trouble getting to sleep at night? Are there changes in his school performance? Is he fighting more than he used to, or getting hurt more than he did before? Is a child being too good in an effort to please his mother? Has he started to wet the bed again or is he having other physical symptoms? These are some of the many possible changes in behavior that may appear in a child who is covering up his grief.

The death of a parent, whether it occurs during early childhood, middle childhood, or adolescence, can have a profound effect on the child. The need of a child for working out his feelings should always be kept in mind. We should give him every opportunity to talk about his feelings. Remember, it is better for him to talk about his feelings even if it makes him feel sad, and even if it saddens those about him to see him unhappy. The child will recover better from his loss if he is encouraged to express himself about it.

If a child demonstrates his discomfort in the form of symptoms, we should be aware that suppressed feelings about his parent's death could be the cause of his difficulties. We should ask the child if he misses his parent. We can tell him that when a father or mother dies, children feel upset or angry, and some of them think it is wrong to feel this way. We should tell him that it is not wrong to feel this way and he should try to tell us how he feels about it.

In situations where our talking to a child does not seem to help enough, it may be advisable to seek consultation with a psychiatrist or mental health clinic. A little help early, before the child has repressed his thoughts and feelings about what has happened, may eliminate the need for much more help later.

Suicide

"How did Mom die?" Johnny asked his father.
"She had an accident, son," was the father's answer.
"Then why did the kid across the street tell me that she killed herself?"

DEATH BY suicide creates special problems for remaining family members and friends. When a person dies as a result of illness or accident, most of us are not likely to think that we personally could have prevented his death. But when a person takes his own life we are often plagued with the question of whether we could have prevented it, whether we could have acted differently in some way or done more for him.

When a child's parent commits suicide, we are faced with the problem of what to tell the youngster. At times there may be doubt as to whether the death was accidental or suicide. If the prevailing opinion in the community can be that it was an accident, this reason can be given to the child. At other times, however, there will be no doubt that a person took his own life.

In such a circumstance the remaining parent and other relatives can experience difficulty in telling the child about the death. Perhaps there may be situations where one could almost be sure that a child would never learn the truth if he were given a false explanation of some kind. But more often, as in the example above, the child will eventually learn the true story and he will be shaken by the realization that he did not hear it from his own parent. As in most cases, the best policy is to tell the child the truth.

If a child is very young at the time of the suicide, he might simply be told that his mother has died. Older children should be told that the parent killed herself. The child may ask, "Why did she do this? Didn't she love us? Why would she leave us alone like this?"

Some of the child's concerns are similar to those already discussed in relation to children whose parents have died of natural causes. But we are also faced with the almost unanswerable question, "Why did she kill herself?" Sometimes a child will be told that the mother must have been sick to do this. Unless "sick" is explained to the child, however, he may be left confused and wondering whether he was responsible for making his mother sick. Often, a depressed parent who later commits suicide may have acted in a morose or detached fashion which the child interpreted as Mother being angry with him.

It is extremely difficult to answer a child's questions about suicide. Yet we must try to give him an explanation. He should be told that his parent killed herself. We may tell him that we do not know why this came to pass. We can tell him that his mother must have had some troubles or worries that she did not tell anyone about. We should stress to the child that even though his mother was a good person, killing oneself is not a good way, and not the right way, to solve your troubles.

A youngster may want to know more about the dead parent's troubles. He may fear that his mother's difficulties can be inherited by him. We should tell him that he will not inherit his mother's worries. We should tell him that everyone feels unhappy at times: when sad things occur, it is normal to be depressed. But if a person gets so unhappy that he keeps thinking he wants to kill himself, he should tell someone how he feels. He can tell his parent, another relative, a clergyman, a doctor, or any other person in whom he has confidence. The youngster should be told that there are doctors who can help a person who feels extremely depressed and who does not know what to do about it.

CHAPTER VI

Adoption

Telling the Child

Twelve-year-old Carl looked as if he were about to cry. His mother asked him, "What's the matter, son?"

"Nothing," he answered, looking down at the floor.

"Please tell me. You look so unhappy."

Then Carl blurted out, "Why didn't you tell me I was adopted?"

It is often assumed that bringing up an adopted child presents no more problems than those which occur in any parent-child relationship. This is rarely, if ever, true. Adoptive parents cannot completely forget the fact that their child was not born to them. They also must tell the child that he is adopted and this may make some difference to them.

Unfortunately, there may still be parents who do not tell a child that he is adopted. A few are too uncomfortable to discuss it with the youngster. Others feel that the child will be more secure if he does not know he has been adopted.

A child will usually learn of his adopted status sooner or later. He may overhear the conversations of friends or relatives. He may discover the information in letters or other papers. Even if he does not discover the fact that he is adopted directly, he may sense something in his relationship with his parents that he does not understand.

A youngster will probably be very angry if he learns of his adoption from anyone other than his parents. Besides being resentful, he will find it difficult to trust his parents (or others) if he feels they have been dishonest about a matter of such importance to him. In general, all children need to be able to feel that they can trust what their parents tell them.

Adopted children should always be told by their parents

that they are adopted. They should hear this from their parents before they can learn of it from someone else. For most parents it should be helpful to use the word "adopted" in talking to the child when he is one to two years old. Of course, he may not understand when he hears his mother say, "You're our beautiful adopted baby," but this use of the word will make it easier to explain the meaning to him as he gets older. Saying this, or something similar, can help the parents to be more comfortable when telling a child of his adopted status when he can more readily understand.

A child of three or four years can be told that Mother and Father adopted him when he was an infant. When he asks what the word "adopted" means, we can tell him that we wanted a child very much and could not have one. We went to a place where they arranged for us to get him, and he became our son.

The older he gets, the more information he is likely to want about his adoption and about the background of his natural parents. When a child is adopted, the adopting parents should get information from the adoption agency that will help them later in telling their child about his background. Sometimes it may be better to tell a child more rather than less. As with many situations related to telling things to children, when children are not given honest answers they may imagine something far worse than the truth. Parents should be sure that the facts they give the child are true ones, so that he will not hear details from others which are different from those his parents have given him.

As the child becomes an adolescent, he will question his background more closely. When we give an adopted child information about his biological parents, we should let him know that they were good people who for particular reasons were not able to keep him, even though they may have wanted to keep him.

For example, a teen-ager can be told that his parents were very young when they had him. While biologically they were able to have a child, they were not really ready for the responsibility of being parents. They realized this, and for the baby's sake they let him be adopted. He can also be told that his adoptive parents very much wanted a child and are happy to have him as their son.

The adopted person has to contend with the feeling that he was abandoned, but we can try to help him by portraying his natural parents in a positive manner.

Sometimes children who have been told they were adopted cannot ask their parents for more information. In spite of their reluctance to ask, they often would like to know more. Parents should be alert to this possibility and offer the child an opportunity to ask about his origins. The parent might say, "Lots of adopted children may wonder about what the mother was like who had them. Are you curious about this? Because if you would like to know we will try to answer your questions with whatever information we have available."

There are instances where adopted children think they are not as good as other youngsters. They should be told that being adopted does not in any way mean that they are not as good as other children.

Parents should not have the mistaken notion that an adopted child will have a more secure feeling if he does not know he is adopted. If a husband and wife have a good relationship with each other and the child grows up in an atmosphere where he is handled with love, kindness, firmness, and consistency, he will have a feeling of security. How he feels about his parents and the way they treat him and each other will be much more important than the fact that they were not his biological parents.

An adolescent may attempt to find his natural mother. Even if he wants to do this, it does not mean that he feels she would be a better mother than his adoptive mother. In fact, in most instances where adopted people meet their natural parents, the adoptive parents remain the ones who are considered to be the real parents.

The facts about a child's adoption should be discussed within the immediate family. The adopted child usually wants this to be done, but he probably does not want it talked about very much with other relatives and friends.

Parents need not keep secret the fact that a youngster is adopted. Nor should they go around introducing him with, "We want you to meet our adopted son." The child should know he is adopted, but there is no reason why he cannot be introduced by saying "We want you to meet our son."

Telling the Child About Conception

Six-year-old Evan knew that he was adopted. He knew that his parents had chosen him when he was a baby because they wanted him.

One afternoon he came in from play and said to his mother, "I want to know something. Where do babies come from and where did I come from?"

ADOPTIVE PARENTS may have little difficulty telling a young child that he is adopted, but they may feel unsure and uncomfortable when he comes to them with questions related to conception and birth.

Reasons for this uneasiness may vary. Some people may have trouble explaining these facts to their youngster regardless of whether he is a natural or adopted child. Other mothers may be uncomfortable because they have not resolved some of their own conflicts.

A woman may have unsettled feelings about the fact that she could not carry a baby in her own uterus and give birth to him. She may feel that she has been a failure. This may make it difficult for her to tell the adopted child that he grew within someone else's body.

Many adopted children are illegitimate. When a child asks where babies come from, the parent may have a great deal of anxiety about answering. She may be unsure of how to tell him the facts related to his origin. Some adoptive parents may feel that their child's natural parents were immoral for having had a child out of wedlock. Of course, people with such ideas probably should not have adopted an illegitimate child in the first place. Be that as it may, these sentiments create difficulty for the parents when the child comes with questions having to do with sexual matters. They should remember that it is extremely important to answer the youngster's questions and not make him feel he has been wrong to ask.

When a child becomes curious about his beginnings, he should be answered honestly. He should be told that he grew in his biological mother's abdomen just as everybody grew inside of a mother. If he then asks how a baby is conceived, he should be told. Elsewhere in this book are more details about answering a child's questions related to conception and birth.

A child who has a good relationship with his parents may become upset when he learns that he did not grow in his adoptive mother's body. He may say, "I wish that I grew inside of you." His mother can tell him she also wishes that this had been the case, but since she was not able to have a baby grow within her, she was happy to get him. She can tell him she wanted him and she loves him just as much as she would if he had grown in her body.

As the child gets older, he will wonder about the marital status of his natural parents. In situations where the parents were married, he should be told that they were; if his parents were not married, he will have to work out his feelings about this sooner or later. His adoptive parents can also tell him that the fact of his biological parents' not having married does not in any way make him an inferior person. A child will believe this if his adoptive parents have had a good relationship with him and he has already developed a picture of himself as a worthwhile individual.

The Angry Adopted Child

Arnold's mother had punished him for disobeying her. He became very angry and said, "You're not my real mother. I don't have to listen to what you say."

JUST AS all children will sometimes become angry with their parents, so will the adopted child.

Arnold actually has a very good relationship with his adoptive parents. They adopted him at four weeks of age, and they love him as much as parents can love a child. They provide him with many material possessions, but they also provide him with a good set of values and rules. And they discipline him when necessary.

Fortunately, Arnold's mother did not feel insecure and was only mildly troubled when he made reference to the fact that she did not give birth to him. In her own mind she translated his statement into "I am angry with you, Mother, because you punished me." She told him that it makes no difference to her that she is not the person in whose body he had grown before he was born. She let him know that in her mind and in her feelings there is no question about the fact that she is his mother and he is her son, and she loves him enough to discipline him when she should.

Adoptive parents might anticipate a situation where their angry child tells them, "You're not really my mother" or "You're not my real father." Most of these parents will feel very hurt when they hear their child say this. In most instances they have been excellent parents to their adopted child.

They should realize that every youngster sometimes gets angry with his parents and says things that he later regrets. An angry child may say to his natural parents, "You don't really like me. You act like I'm not your child." These parents will not doubt that they, in fact, are the child's parents. But adoptive parents cannot completely forget the fact that they were not the child's biological parents. Therefore, they may feel very troubled and perhaps angry when the child tells them they are not his parents.

Should this occur, it would be wise for them to deal with it as Arnold's mother did. They should remember that even though the child says this, he probably feels close to them most of the time and he does feel that they are his real parents. The adoptive parent who feels very angry at a time like this should try to control his own anger. He should keep in mind that he is dealing with an upset, angry child and not with another adult. Besides telling the youngster some of the things that Arnold's mother told her son, the parent should also give the child permission for being angry. He should be told that it is all right to be angry with his parents just as they are angry with him when he does something that they do not approve of. He can be told that his father and mother remember when they felt angry with their parents. He should also be told that nothing will happen to his parents because he is angry with them and nothing will happen to him.

Sometimes children are told that they should be so thankful for having been adopted. Youngsters usually resent hearing this, and rightfully so. It was not their fault that their parents could not keep them, and except for the few who were relatively old at the time of adoption, children did not have a voice in the decision of whether they would be adopted.

Problems may also arise when a family has both natural and adopted children. The adopted child may feel that the natural children are treated better, no matter whether this is actually so. Probably, in some instances, parents bend over backward to treat the adopted child better.

Should an adopted child say that he is not being treated as well as the other children, the parent should not immediately try to defend himself. He may not get very far if he tries to reason with the child and give him examples to prove that this is not true. It would be better simply to tell the child that his parents understand that he would feel that way since he was adopted and his siblings were not, but that they love them all and believe they are treating them all fairly. And most important, they must prove it by their actions.

The Adopted Child's Fear of Abandonment

Anne, who was now nine years old, had been adopted in infancy. Her parents were much older than the parents of her friends. Six months ago, her father had suffered a mild heart attack. Two months ago, Anne became apprehensive whenever her parents went out in the evening without her.

One afternoon while walking with her mother she asked, "Mother, who will take care of me if anything happens to you and Dad?"

ANY CHILD may have fears about being abandoned by his parents, but the adopted child will have special worries related to this. No matter what he is told about his natural parents, he will have to face the fact that they did not keep him. If he has any idea that something about himself was the cause of his abandonment, his adoptive parents should attempt to correct this erroneous opinion. The child should be assured that he is, and always was, a worthwhile human being.

Parents of an adopted child should be mindful of the possibility that he will have anxiety about being abandoned again. They should avoid statements that might aggravate this feeling in the child. For instance, parents when frustrated or angry with their youngster may say, "If you don't shape up we'll have to send you away to boarding school or military school." These threats are inadvisable when dealing with any child, but especially with an adopted child, who already may feel that his natural parents rid themselves of him. Such a child needs to be told that his present parents want him and will keep him, rather than that he may be sent away.

Anne, who was adopted by older parents, has special problems. Since it is obvious to her that her parents are older than those of her peers, she is concerned that they may die and leave her alone. This fear increased after her father had a heart attack. She became more anxious and had trouble going to sleep. She also began to stay close to her parents and was reluctant to allow them to get out of her sight.

In a situation like this, the child should be given information that would answer the question of "Who will take care of me?" Not only parents of adopted children but all parents, as mentioned earlier, should make plans that would answer this need to know in their children. The parents should decide who would be their choice to raise their youngsters if anything should happen to both parents. This should be spelled out in their will.

While this substitute figure is important for all children, it is of special significance to an adopted child with his built-in fear of abandonment. When a child shows the concern that Anne did, she should be told that Mother and Father hope and expect to live and take care of her until she is grown up and on her own. However, if anything should happen to them, they have arranged that a particular relative or friend, whom she knows, will take care of her and act as substitute parents.

When Anne's parents reassured her about these things, she became much less fearful and was again able to enjoy her daily life.

Heredity, Environment, and the Adopted Child

As the students entered Professor Alden's class they noticed a boy about ten years old, sitting in the back of the room. He was wearing a bow tie and his actions were similar to the professor's.

One of the students went up to the teacher and said, "That must be your son. He looks just like you."

"Thank you," said the beaming Dr. Alden. "Yes, he's my boy."

NOAH ALDEN impressed everyone with his similarity to his father. He wore a bow tie just like his father did. He walked like his father, and when he talked he motioned with his hands in the same way as the professor. The students were very surprised when they learned later that Noah was adopted.

Many adopted children give the impression that they look like their adoptive parents. In the course of their development they pick up parental habits and mannerisms and copy them without being conscious of it.

The question of hereditary versus environmental influences is one which we often think about relative to all human beings. It becomes more significant when we are considering the problems of adoption.

Adoptive parents cannot completely forget the fact that their child was not born to them. If a natural offspring develops unsuitable patterns of behavior, we cannot blame this on his having inherited these characteristics from some mother or father we do not know. It is true that Mother can blame it on Father's side of the family or vice versa. But this will not present the same opportunity for avoiding responsibility as attributing the difficulty to inheritance from the adopted child's natural parents.

Some people may believe strongly that personality makeup is inherited, and that not much can be done to change it. Literary works have been written on the theme that an adopted child, brought up by excellent parents, can become a criminal solely because of characteristics inherited from a grandparent. My work with parents and children has convinced me that this does not occur. Many other factors are involved in the relationship between the adoptive parents and child that can explain the development of abnormal behavior in the youngster.

It is almost impossible to settle the arguments that go on between the proponents of the effects of environment, and those who attribute everything to heredity. Elements of both can affect a child's development. Children may inherit a tendency to be awkward or a tendency to be well coordinated. Some babies seem to be passive from birth, and others are more aggressive. Not every child in a family will inherit the same characteristics, however.

Whatever the child's inherent constitutional makeup, his personality development will still be markedly affected by the interaction between himself and his parents and siblings. He will also be influenced by other important people, such as teachers and playmates, that he relates to as he is growing up.

A father whose wife had died was describing his daughter's personality to me. He said she was argumentative, flew off the handle readily, was impulsive in many ways, and in general had the same characteristics as his deceased wife. Listening to him I might have believed that all this was due to heredity had I not known that he and his wife had adopted the girl as an infant.

Another set of parents had two adopted children. These youngsters were nine and ten years of age when I first met them. The boy was doing well in school and seemingly tried to please his parents as much as possible. The girl was cold to them and constantly got into trouble. She was the one brought for treatment. She was a difficult child to reach and improved only slightly as a result of therapy. Eventually she was sent to a specialized school where she could also receive psychiatric treatment. The parents never considered that the boy needed treatment.

During the period of childhood the adoptive mother of these children insisted that the reason the girl was having trouble was that she came of "poor stock" while the boy came from a better background. Both had been adopted as infants. The children are grown now. The girl has improved and is doing fairly well. The boy who, according to the parents, had been the "good" child, has been in a great deal of trouble and at last reports was estranged from his family.

People who believe strongly in heredity should not adopt children. The above situation illustrates the tendency of some people to attribute positive or negative aspects of a child's behavior to heredity, rather than to the type of relationship we establish and maintain with our children. If we believe wholeheartedly that heredity is uppermost then we would have to be extremely pessimistic about effecting any change at all in the personality development of human beings. It is unfair to adopt a child if we have such a view. Even if we know that his parents were decent individuals, we might attribute bad behavior on the part of the child to inheritance from previous generations.

A child may ask us whether he has inherited anything from his natural mother or father. We can tell him that he inherited the color of his eyes and hair or certain aspects of his body build. We should not tell him that his behavior characteristics result from heredity. We can tell him that, while he has inherited physical attributes from his biological parents, he has developed important personality characteristics because of his relationship with us. We should assure him that we like him and value him because he is our child.

CHAPTER VII

Separation and Divorce

Introduction

DIVORCE IS not fun. Divorce is rarely friendly. Divorce represents failure. Divorce is usually a frustrating experience for the partners involved and can be a frightening, destructive experience for their children.

There are instances when children would be better off if their parents separated. A home in which nothing is heard but bickering and bitterness can be worse for a child than living with one parent after a divorce. A situation where parents have had many separations and reconciliations may be worse than a divorce. The children must live with the fear that their family could break up again at any time.

But it is a rare child who actually wants his parents to be divorced, no matter how badly things are going in their home. Children are the innocent bystanders in a divorce and, too often, the innocent victims of their parents' poor behavior and misguided actions during the proceedings.

It is extremely difficult when husband or wife is blaming the other for the failure of their marriage to stop and think of the effects on the children. Yet, the feelings and needs of the children must be considered. Have the parents tried to "step back and look" at things from the standpoint of their being a family? Have they been willing to swallow their pride and consult with someone who was not directly involved emotionally, in order to determine if the family integrity could be preserved? One gets the feeling that in our time too little attention is paid to the "life" of the family as opposed to the immediate satisfaction of desires in the individual's own life. Have the parents made honest attempts to negotiate their differences?

There can be disadvantages of staying together for the sake

of the children. The children do not benefit when one parent feels only hostility toward them because he or she is maintaining the marriage just because of the children. If parents stay together because of consideration for their children, they should also make every effort to resolve their own problems. When divorce is inevitable, it is important to remember that the children can be seriously affected. It is the parents' responsibility to inform the children of what is going on. In doing this the parents, hopefully, will take into account some of the possible areas that will produce problems for the children.

In the pages that follow some of the potential difficulties are discussed. With an understanding of these possible problems, the parents who are being divorced could decide how best to inform the children of what is happening and what plans have been made to protect the children's interest during this trying period.

It is hoped that the parents will avoid behaving in ways that will aggravate the difficulties that children experience during the breaking up of their family. It is senseless to tell youngsters that we love them and care about them if our actions tell them a different story.

Telling Children About Divorce

"Why did Daddy leave us, Mommy?"
"I really can't tell you, Warren."
"I must have been a bad boy or he wouldn't have left us like this."

GUILT IS a feeling that we all experience at times. On occasion it is appropriate to feel guilty; for example, when we do something wrong to another person and realize what we have done.

When parents divorce it is not their children's fault. Yet, many a child feels that his parents have separated because of his behavior or wishes. Children, especially young ones, think in magical ways. They believe that mere wishes, good or evil, can come true. Often events seem to substantiate these ideas. If an angry child wishes that his parent would get hurt and within a few days the parent, coincidentally, has a fall and injures himself, the child may be convinced that his wishes have great power. He then considers himself the agent who caused his father's injury.

When a husband and wife are involved in marital battles, they often lose sight of the fact that their behavior has an effect on their youngsters. A father may say in a moment of frustration and anger, "I can't stand it around this house anymore." His children, hearing this statement, will not necessarily think that Father is referring to his problems with Mother. The children may believe that he cannot stand their behavior, and if Father leaves they will feel responsible.

Another factor becomes important when children feel guilty about their parents' divorce. In observing the emotional development of children, one notes stages of attraction and attachment to the parent of the opposite sex. Along with this, children often find themselves with antagonistic feelings toward, and fear of, the parent of the same sex. In normal development this situation is most prominent between three and six years of age. From six to twelve years it is usually not so evident, and during adolescence it may recur.

A boy may actively wish that his father was out of the picture so that he can have his mother's attention to himself. A girl may say, "Daddy, why don't you marry me instead of Mommy?" Ideally, each child will find that he or she does not take the place of the parent of the same sex. When this fact becomes clear, the boy will identify with his father and try to be like him. The girl will pattern herself on her mother.

When a parent is removed from the picture through divorce or death, however, the child who has not worked out the competition with his father may experience guilt feelings. He believes that he is responsible for having his wish fulfilled that the father be eliminated from the contest. The child may feel that he is bad and it is his fault that his father is leaving.

It is extremely important to give children an explanation about separation and divorce. This is true regardless of whether or not the children are aware of the emotional turmoil that has existed in the marriage.

With the children's welfare in mind, the parents should attempt calmly to explain about the divorce. Too often, children do not learn of the impending breakup until a parent screams out the information in the heat of an argument, "I'm leaving and I'm not coming back."

If possible, the child should be told by both parents that his mother and father are going to be living apart, and later they will be divorced—which means they will no longer be married to each other. If more than one child is involved, each one should be told by both parents, but not in the presence of the other siblings. The reason for this is that children of different ages may have different types of questions to ask their parents.

The youngster should be reassured that both parents love him and will continue to be interested in his welfare even though the parents no longer want to live together. (And hopefully they will conduct themselves in a manner that will give real meaning to these words.) It must be made very clear to the children that they are not at fault and are not to blame for their parents' problems. Neither their behavior nor their wishes have anything to do with the fact that their parents will no longer be living together as husband and wife.

Parents who tell children that there is going to be a separation and divorce should be prepared for the possibility that their offspring will cry, or in various ways beg them to stay together. Presumably the husband and wife who have reached the point of telling the children have definitely decided on divorce. So, if the children are greatly upset at the news of the separation, the parents should, as calmly as possible under the circumstances, let the children know that the decision, no longer to be married, has to be solely that of the parents. They are the only ones who are responsible for the decision, and the children cannot and will not be responsible for it.

It is extremely helpful if, by the time the children are told about the divorce, the parents have been able to come to rational conclusions about living arrangements for the family so that the youngsters will know whom they will be living with, how often they will see the absent parent, and whatever other information that would help in decreasing the degree of insecurity that practically all children experience when their family breaks up.

Don't Ask the Children

"Your father and I are getting a divorce," said Mrs. Casey to her children. "We want to be fair with you, so we're asking you to decide something. Whom do you want to live with?"

CHILDREN SHOULD not be asked for an opinion as to whether or not their parents should get a divorce. Neither should a choice of whom they will live with be left to them, especially if they are younger than the middle or late teens. Parents may have the best of intentions when they tell the children to make this decision. They are nonetheless placing an unreasonable burden on their youngsters.

A child who is told to decide whose home he wants to live in may feel he is being asked to show where his loyalty is. He is also being told to take on a responsibility which belongs to his parents.

The parents should decide which home will be better for the children. Then the youngsters should be told definitely where they are to live. If a child objects to the arrangements, he should be told that, even though his parents are separating, they both have his interest at heart and have made their decision on this basis.

Occasionally, both parents want custody of their children. They may decide to divide them and have some live with the mother and others with the father. One set of parents arranged that the boys would live with Father and the girls with Mother.

It is difficult enough for children to put up with a separation from one of their parents. We should not compound this by also removing them from their siblings, unless this is a matter of absolute necessity. This is true even if there is a great deal of sibling rivalry, and a parent might be relieved to have the children separated.

If, for realistic reasons, such as the emotional or physical health of the parents, some division of the children becomes imperative, the child should be told why he is going to live with a particular parent and why his siblings are to remain with the other. It should be made clear to him that the decision is not based on any fault of his, but rather on whatever considerations make the separation from his siblings necessary.

A parent may feel better, or less lonely, if he has one of his offspring with him. But this is of secondary importance. The welfare of the child comes first. When all the children are kept together it lessens the naturally disruptive effect on their lives which occurs with separation and divorce. There will be no cause for any child to wonder why he and not the others was to live with one parent rather than the other. It is a more nearly normal situation for all siblings to remain together.

Too-Friendly Parents

Seven-year-old Betty's father had come to take her out on Sunday. Her parents were separated and awaiting a divorce. Betty waited while her mother and father were having a drink together and talking amiably to each other. After awhile she said to them, "If you're so happy together, why are you getting a divorce?"

CHILDREN DO not want their parents to be divorced. Usually, much bad feeling exists between marital partners prior to the separation and it persists afterward. Occasionally, however, parents decide to behave in an extremely friendly manner toward each other for the sake of the children. Sometimes the whole family goes out to dinner together on the day Father visits. In other instances, as with Betty's family, the parents have a drink, or coffee, together and seem to enjoy one another's company.

Such behavior can be very confusing to the child. She may be pleased to notice that her mother and father are no longer fighting. But she will wonder, as Betty did, why they are getting divorced if they can appear to be so happy together.

A child usually wants her separated parents to be reunited. When the couple, in the presence of the youngster, behave toward each other in a very friendly fashion she will begin to believe her wishes may come true. Since this probably will not be the case, the child will suffer a needless disappointment.

When there is a separation prior to divorce, it is much better if the parents conduct themselves in a way that does not encourage the fantasies of reunion in the minds of their children. This does not mean that they should continue to argue, or that they should not treat each other in a civil manner in the presence of their offspring. But their behavior should strengthen the idea of being separated. In this way they will be telling the children that the separation is definite. Even though the children may not like it, this is how things are, and how they will remain.

The parent who comes to pick up his children should do this in a matter-of-fact manner. Too often, because of ill feeling a father may not be permitted to come into the house or apartment of the mother on visitation days. This type of behavior is also bad for the youngsters to observe. It tells them their parents are acting like uncontrolled children rather than adults.

We would hope that children could observe moderate behavior on the part of their separated parents. In front of their children, parents can treat each other decently without putting on a show of being overly friendly.

Occasionally, separated or divorced partners entertain the idea of remarriage. If possible, I would recommend that, until they are fairly sure of the reconciliation, they have their meetings and discussions without their children knowing about it. This is especially true if the youngsters are not yet in their late teens. It is terribly unfair to children to hope for a reunion of their parents and then be disappointed when it does not happen.

Constancy of Visitation

Willard's father, who had not visited him on the past two Sundays, arrived to take him out for the day. When he saw his father, Willard said, "Dad, you used to come every week. What happened? Are you mad at me?"

WHEN PARENTS are separated, the children generally remain with the mother. Fathers who were close to their youngsters before the breakup of the family want to see them as much as they can. Even fathers who spent little time with their children before the separation will, for a variety of reasons, strongly insist on visitation rights. As a matter of fact, a child may see more of his father after the separation than before.

Whether from a feeling of loneliness or guilt and remorse, in the initial period after the separation Father will religiously appear on his weekly, or even more frequent, visitation day. The child comes to expect this. He looks forward to seeing his parent and enjoys the visit with him.

As time goes by, the father may find the frequent visitations an unwelcome chore. He would rather be out playing golf as he did when he lived with the family. Or he may meet a woman in whom he becomes interested. Then he will be torn between his attraction to her and his obligation to his child. The son, who has grown accustomed to seeing his father every Sunday, will be told he is unable to come. Or the boy will wait in vain if Father fails to show up without sending word. The child feels hurt and angry.

This situation can and should be prevented. It may be difficult for the parent, who will not be living with the children, to plan ahead. Often he is too involved with his own feelings to be thinking of what the future will bring. Nevertheless, it is important to make himself think about the question of visits with his youngsters.

A father should attempt to set up a plan of visitation that he will be likely to stick to in the foreseeable future. He should try not to allow his feelings of loss, guilt, remorse, or competition with his wife to affect decisions about the frequency of his visits with his children. He should remember that if he comes and calls often in the beginning of the separation, his youngsters have every right to expect this pattern to continue.

It would be much better for a father to visit less frequently if there is any question in his mind about keeping it up later. We know decisions are often made on an emotional basis at the time of separation or divorce. We still must ask fathers to anticipate possible developments and not set their children up for future disappointments.

A father may be leaving the home and his child says, "Promise me you'll come to see me every week." He should be told that, even though Dad loves him very much, they will have to see how often he will be able to visit him.

There is nothing wrong with frequent visits providing they do not upset the child's daily routines, and providing there is not a great deal of discord between the parents concerning the visits. That is, there is nothing wrong if these visits will be maintained in a regular way, and not suddenly be markedly decreased because of the parent's other obligations or inclinations.

Sometimes, and with the best of intentions, a father may get into a position where he must decrease the frequency of visits. He should tell the child the reasons for this, and also tell him that the reduction is not in any way due to the child's behavior.

Meaningful Visits

Larry and Mary returned from the weekly visiting day with their father. Mother met them as they came in the door and asked, "Did you have a good day?"

"It was rotten," Larry answered. "Dad doesn't pay much attention to us when we visit."

A DIVORCED parent may come regularly but the visits may be very unsatisfactory from the children's standpoint.

Some parents genuinely want to be with their offspring. They may err by making each visit too much of a festive occasion, but they are conscientious in devoting the day to the youngsters. Other parents may be maintaining a tie with the children mainly out of a sense of obligation or guilt. They arrive and pick up the children but are not really spending their time with them.

A father may pick up his child and take him along while he visits an adult friend, male or female. If the child is lucky there may be other children in the neighborhood for him to play with. Otherwise he may be planted in front of a television set to keep him occupied; or he may just have to sit and listen to adult conversation without being a part of it.

The maintenance of a continuing relationship between them should be the essential reason for a separated parent to visit with his child. A boy should be able to look up to his dad as a suitable model. The father should want his son to be familiar with his views and his sense of values. If these objectives are to be accomplished, visitation days should be meaningful. It is ridiculous to go through a ritual of coming to get a child regularly and then not really spending any time with him. When we do this we are implying to the youngster that we do not actually enjoy his company. The child who is dragged along and then sits by and does nothing will wonder why his father is not interested in him.

Most parents use discretion in their behavior around their children. Occasionally, however, a separated parent may have his child accompany him and a female companion on what is essentially an adult date. The youngster may be exposed to varying degrees of displays of physical affection between his father and the woman with him. If the child is spending the night with his father, he may be aware that the two adults are sleeping in the same bed. Parents should realize that their children may become upset when exposed to such activity. A child can have very mixed-up feelings, especially if his mother is not having any social life.

We are not suggesting that children of divorce should not know that there is the possibility of either parent becoming interested in someone else and eventually remarrying. In fact, if a youngster says to a parent, "I don't want you to go out on dates," he should be told this is the business of each parent. We can tell him we understand that he, like most other children, wishes his mother and father would get back together, but this is not going to happen and each parent must decide if he or she wants to go out with other people.

However, divorced parents should be discreet about dating and sexual activity. Young preschool children will not understand what it is all about. Older children may imagine more is happening than is actually going on. By being careful about behavior in the presence of their offspring, each parent can help prevent unnecessary additional emotional discomfort in these youngsters who have already suffered through the divorce.

Sometimes a divorced mother will have gone out steadily with a series of different men. If a man spends a lot of time in the home, the children can become attached to him, and then they will suffer repeated disappointments as each of Mother's relationships breaks up.

One little girl's mother has been divorced twice. She has a half-brother from mother's first marriage living in the household. Currently her mother has a male friend who spends considerable time in the home. One day this six-year-old daughter told her mother, "I know what marriage is. The lady has the babies. The children live with her and the man goes someplace else to live." This is an example of the type of thinking a child may engage in, and here was a situation where only a limited number of males was involved. A mother should tell such a child that many people stay married to just one person, and it is not because of children being born that mothers and fathers get divorced.

There are instances when a parent has to take steps to prohibit a child from visiting the other parent, even if it takes a court order to do this. Unfortunately, some people are too open about their sexual activity with their children present.

Others are unable to control their drinking and are often intoxicated while the youngsters are visiting. Infrequently, fathers lose control of themselves and fondle teen-age daughters.

If visits have to be stopped for these or similar reasons and the child asks, "Why can't I see my father anymore?" he should be told that the visits could not continue because the father did not behave properly.

When a mother finds out that a father has engaged a child in some type of sexual activity, it is important, if possible, to find out what the child's feelings may be in relation to the occurrence. The youngster should be told that Father's behavior was wrong, but it was not the fault of the child. In general, if a child who gets along fairly well most of the time with the absent parent comes home in an upset state, we should try to determine what has happened during the visit.

To Win Is To Lose

Michael returned home on Saturday night after spending his weekly visitation day with his father.

"Gee, Mom," he said, "I went bowling with Dad and I beat him again."

THE ABSENT parent in a separation or divorce may feel he is at a disadvantage. He usually sees the child only one day a week. Because of the relative infrequency of his contact with the youngster, he may try to arrange it so that the visits are all fun.

The visitation day becomes a weekly holiday. The child is entertained with movies, ball games, dining out, or activities such as bowling. The parent may have feelings of guilt, or feelings of competition with the other parent. Because of this he may shower the child with money and gifts. All of this may be quite out of keeping with what had been done for the child when the family was intact.

The absent parent may permit the child to do whatever he wants to do and not set any limits for him. He excuses his permissiveness by thinking, "After all, why should I make my child unhappy when I only see him for such a short time each week." The youngster may start to feel as if anything goes with his father, and may carry over some of this behavior to the daily relationship with his mother.

Something that often happens is illustrated above in young Michael's remark to his mother. Michael was a boy who enjoyed athletic activity. His father, a good athlete, played games with him and took him bowling. Michael would always win.

Michael's father, by his handling of this situation, was not telling his son the truth. He was letting the boy believe that he actually could beat his father consistently in these contests. Michael, in his relationships with his peers, began to feel something was wrong if he did not win every game from his friends.

What was occurring between Michael and his father can be a problem for many fathers and sons. It is more likely to occur in the case of a separated parent who is trying too hard to make the visiting day a happy one.

In playing a game with his child, a father need not compete with the zeal he would use with his own peers. Nevertheless, he is physically stronger than the child, and it would be the exception where a pre-teen youngster could compete on anything approaching an equal footing. When the son is permitted to win all the time, he may erroneously believe he possesses Superman qualities, or he may wonder *why* his father allows him to win constantly. Some children may not express it, but they will be inwardly angry at Father for "throwing" the game.

The same may be true of board games played with children. Here, however, it is sometimes possible for a parent to permit a child to win without it being obvious that he was permitting it. But, it would not be right purposely to allow the youngster to win all the time, or even most of the time.

If a parent acts as he should and usually wins in a game of bowling, his child may become upset and say, "Why do you always win?" This boy should be told that Dad wins because he is bigger and stronger and has probably had more practice at this activity. We can also tell a boy that he will grow bigger and stronger, and the time will come when he will win more often. If he is angry because he loses, we should not tease him about this. We can tell him we understand that no one likes to lose even though there are realistic reasons why a boy cannot beat his father very often.

Most of us can be sure that, sooner than seems likely, our offspring's developing skills combined with our advancing age will enable them legitimately to outdo us where physical ability is involved.

Other than the matter of competition in games, other aspects of visitation days need to be considered. Efforts should be made to put the relationship between parent and child on a basis that is not just fun and games. As with any other child, the separated parent should set limits, and should be willing to permit the youngster to be angry when he does not get his way. It is not healthy for a child to develop the idea that being with Father is all fun and only Mother does not give you everything you want.

If a father does not fill a request, the child may say, "You mustn't love me." The parent who has left the family may be quite sensitive to such a remark. However, he should answer by telling the child that his love for him is not measured by whether he gives him everything he asks for. In fact, the youngster should be told that a good parent must let a child know he loves him enough not to give in to every demand, even though this may make his son angry.

Occasionally, the shoe is on the other foot. The child's mother may be a person who has trouble saying "No" to him all during the week. This may anger the father, and on visiting days he may react by being extremely firm or punitive with the child. This behavior may result from anger at his former wife's way of doing things; or it may stem from an honest feeling that he must compensate for the poor handling his child receives during the week.

But whatever the reasons for such a father's behavior, it is no better to go to this extreme than it is to be setting no limits at all on visitation day. If a father is bothered by a mother's lack of discipline (or vice versa) an attempt should be made, when the offspring are not present, to have the other parent modify the handling of limit-setting. When this cannot be accomplished and the child complains, "Why don't you let me have what I want the way Mommy does?" he should be told that both parents have a different outlook on these matters. He will have to follow Father's rules when he is with him, and Mother's when he is with her.

Caught in the Middle

"What has your mother been doing?" Mr. Graham asked his seven-year-old son, Joe, on their visitation day. "Has she been going out much in the evening?"

"Mom said I'm not supposed to say anything to you about what happens in our house," answered Joe.

THE DIALOGUE between Joe and his father presents us with several undesirable interactions between separated or divorced parents and their child.

The boy finds himself in the middle. He is forced to struggle with the problem of which parent should have his loyalty. Whose request should he honor? Does he answer his father's questions about what Mother is doing? Or does he follow his mother's orders to say nothing to Father about what goes on at home?

Children are upset by such conflict. One six-year-old son of divorced parents was seen for psychiatric consulation. He was asked what he would wish for if he could have anything changed in the past, present, or future, or if he could get anything he wanted. Although his mother was remarried and his father was considering remarriage, the boy wished his mother and father were married to each other again. Such a wish is not unusual for youngsters from broken homes. However, when this boy was asked why he wished this even though he knew his mother was married again, he said, "Then they wouldn't fight and blame it on me like they do now."

As has been noted over and over again, children are the innocent victims of their parents' marital problems and subsequent separation and divorce. Rather than add to the harmful effects of these circumstances, parents should try to set an example of maturity. Of course, when divorce occurs, one or both partners is likely to feel angry and vindictive. Yet parents should try not to allow these feelings to contaminate their individual relationships with their offspring.

Joe's father should not interrogate his son about what goes on in the home. This puts an unnecessary burden on a youngster. We should also remember that a child may be angry at his mother for some reason and may tell us things purposely to put her in a bad light. He may not always be telling the truth, or he may tell only part of a story. Too many divorced mothers and fathers are too ready to believe the worst about their ex-mate.

Joe's mother should not instruct him to be secretive about anything that happens in her household. A mother should conduct herself in such a manner as to set a good example for her child. When she does this, she need not fear anything he says to his father. This child already has enough to contend with without the additional load of enforced secrecy.

In some instances, a mother may not have imposed any rules

as to what a child can tell his father. The youngster may come from his visits and complain that his father is always pumping him for information. The mother can tell this child that he does not have to tell his father anything he does not want to tell. He can also be told that Mother will call Father and suggest that he ask her when he wants to know certain things.

After a divorce, especially when both parents have remarried, the children are frequently exposed to two sets of rules and often to two different value systems. A child may return home from a vacation or an overnight visit and confront his mother with complaints. He will ask why he is not permitted to do things at home that his father allows him to do when he visits. The differences may concern bedtime, allowances, and so forth.

Divorced parents often continue to argue about differing ideas of child rearing. I have seen people who had been divorced for ten or more years, and both remarried, but they are still arguing about what kind of clothes the children should wear, what they should eat, and how they should be disciplined. Each parent blames the other for not doing what is right. The children may experience discomfort because of their parent's continuing disagreements. Or they may exploit the parental discord in order to get what they want. One eleven-year-old, who had misbehaved badly, managed to get his two sets of parents fighting each other over his behavior. They forgot about what he had done and he went off scot-free.

What should the attitudes be when two sets of parents are involved in a child's life? Naturally, it is best for the child if the limits and values in both households are not too divergent. If parents are really mindful of their youngster's welfare, they should discuss the matter and see if it is possible to minimize the differences.

Nonetheless, when two people get divorced, it is often because they have differing views on what is best for themselves and their offspring. Therefore, it may have to be that the children will continue to be exposed to two quite different ways of life in the homes of their divorced parents.

When there is no possibility of parental agreement, the children should be told that the parents recognize the existence of two quite different sets of rules, methods of discipline, and philosophies of life in general. They can tell the youngsters that each parent believes his or her way is the right way. As they get older, the children will have to decide what *they* consider to be the right way. But, for the present, they will have to accept the fact that they must abide by the rules as set up in the particular household where they are residing. For example, if Father permits them to stay up later, that is up to him, but when they return home they will have to follow Mother's orders.

It is much better to let children know that they will have to get along with different rules in each household than for one parent to tell them that the other parent is doing something completely bad or wrong.

In seeing parents and children who are affected by divorce, a psychiatrist wishes there were a foolproof way to protect a child from the bitterness that parents often have toward one another. The youngster becomes the rope in a tug-of-war between Mother and Father.

During the divorce proceedings, testimony of a psychiatrist may be sought by one or both parents. Often the doctor who testifies may have seen the child and only one of the parents and, therefore, he has an incomplete picture of the family situation. Sometimes, important information cannot be presented in court because of legal technicalities. Even if the psychiatrist's opinion is a valid one, judges can tender decisions that seem to disregard the best interest of the child.

When people are divorced and continue to fight each other, the children too frequently become the battleground. Parents who do this tell the child, by their actions, that he is not really important to either of them. The youngster wonders why his parents cannot settle matters related to him in a more peaceful fashion. Or parents may give a child the impression that he is too powerful, since things that have to do with him can make his parents so upset.

When disagreement exists over custody and visitation rights, parents should try to put the welfare of the children before parental desires. When they fight each other over their offspring, they are essentially telling the youngsters to consider themselves pawns in a game, rather than people who are valuable to each of the parents.

If children genuinely do not want to visit the parent, let the parent visit them. For example, a six-year-old girl's mother and father had been divorced when she was three years of age. Her father had had a mental illness and had been hospitalized for two years. He recovered and was very interested in reestablishing a relationship with his daughter. Her mother had remarried a year after the divorce and the child lived with her. The child had been very young at the time of her last contact with her father. Even after becoming reacquainted with him, she was reluctant to leave home to visit him in another city where he resided. This father accepted a recommendation that he make the effort to come and visit the little girl.

We should earnestly ask parents who cannot settle the questions of custody and visitation amicably to seek the advice of a child psychiatrist or other qualified counselor—someone who will see both parents and children and who will offer an opinion based solely on what is best for the children. Hopefully, there will someday be an impartial professional staff attached to courts to furnish service of this kind in all divorces where children are involved.

Be Truthful but Not Vindictive

Roger was four years old when his parents were divorced. Now he was ten and was curious about why they did separate. He went to his mother and asked, "Why did you and Dad get divorced?"

His mother became uncomfortable; instead of answering his question, she said, "You go ask your father."

CHILDREN CAN have many questions in their minds about their parents' relationship and what may have caused them to be divorced. Those who were younger than five or six at the time of the separation will not consciously remember much of what happened. But from the standpoint of their own emotional development they were affected by the events. Boys, especially, may suffer from the absence of their father.

At some point children may become curious about the details of what happened. Roger came to his mother for an explanation. She was unprepared to tell him that his father had become interested in another woman and this was the reason for his leaving. So, instead of trying to explain, she passed the buck by telling him to go ask his father.

Such a situation can arise with a child of any age, not just those who were young at the time of the divorce. When a parent is questioned by her youngster about her former husband or the divorce, she should not tell him to get the answers from his father. A child, hearing this, may believe something horrible must be involved if Mother will not give him an answer. Often he will then be too uncomfortable to pursue the matter further with his dad. He is left to wonder and to draw his own erroneous conclusions. He may think his father did something awful, but will have no way of knowing whether or not this is so.

The parent who is asked the question should try to tell the truth to a child. A mother should use discretion and still not lie to her youngster. Nevertheless, one woman told her eight-year-old daughter that the father was sleeping with another woman and this led to their divorce. This mother was acting on a basis of spite and anger. Her child's best interest would have been served if the mother had been honest without being vindictive. She could have told the child that Father found someone he thought he loved more than he did Mother, and this was the reason for the divorce.

Separation and Divorce   181

Sometimes a mother is so upset at her former husband's behavior (or a father at his former wife's) that she tends to see, or look for, his undesirable characteristics in her child. She may tell her son, "You're just like your father," in a tone of voice which leaves no doubt that he is no good. Or a father may tell his daughter, "You must have gotten that habit from your mother." Parents should realize that they can destroy their children's self-esteem when they disparagingly compare them to the divorced mate. There is also the distinct possibility that the youngster will lose respect for a parent who makes such remarks.

A father may say to his child, "I want you always to think well of your mother so I'm not going to say anything bad about her." The implication of this statement is that there is a great deal he could say if he chose to do so. The father who really wants his child to think well of Mother will not make such remarks. Instead, by treating his ex-wife with respect and behaving toward her in a civilized way, he will tell his son that she is worth thinking well of, even though they are divorced.

Children need to feel that there is someone they can trust. In a broken home it is especially important that children be able to rely on the word of at least one parent. This is a particular reason for being truthful without being vengeful when youngsters ask questions about the other parent.

Sometimes a mother may believe she should create an image of the father as a "good guy" in spite of evidence to the contrary. She may persist in telling her child that his father loves him, even though Father visits rarely or not at all. Perhaps the father may have left the city in order to escape his responsibility for contributing child support. A youngster will not believe his mother or he will be extremely confused by her stories under these circumstances.

A child may say, "Dad mustn't love me if he doesn't care about coming to see me." If Father never showed much interest in him, it is wrong for Mother to maintain that his father really cares for him. Mother can tell the child that, while she does not know why his father acts as he does, she is sure that the child is not responsible for his father's neglect.

In rare instances a father may have been good to a child and attentive before the divorce and then, either abruptly or gradually, he stops visiting him. A youngster in this situation may be troubled by the feeling that he must have done something to cause his father to behave in such a manner. It is extremely important for the mother to tell this child that she, too, does not understand why the father is acting as he is, but she is positive that the child's actions did not cause this.

When a father ceases to maintain contact with a son and the mother has not remarried, she should look for opportunities for the boy to be with older males. Boys' clubs are a possible resource if there is good leadership. A grandfather or other male relative can take an interest and provide a good relationship so that the boy will have some positive male figures he can emulate.

The Need for Security

Jerry's behavior had become worse since his mother and father were divorced. His second-grade teacher reported he would not sit still in class and was not doing his work.

His mother was at her wit's end. She became angry and said to him, "Jerry, I'll have to send you to live with your father. I can't control you."

WHEN JERRY reacted to the breakup of his family with uncontrolled behavior, he created problems not only for himself but also for his mother. She was already feeling frustrated and angry at having the main responsibility for the child's care. In her anger she indicated her sense of inadequacy by telling him that she might send him to his father. Generally, when mothers make such statements, they rarely intend to follow through with the action.

What are some of the feelings a boy like Jerry may be experiencing? When the family is disrupted by divorce, a child is apt to feel very uncomfortable about the separation from the parent who has left the home. He will also feel that he is losing someone. This is particularly true if his father had been genuinely interested in him, and had maintained a good relationship with him.

As mentioned earlier, a youngster may feel some guilt at his father's leaving since the child may have, on some occasion, wished for this to happen. There are instances when a child may blame his mother for the father's departure, regardless of what actual circumstances were involved in the divorce. He may misbehave because of this anger he feels toward his mother. He may also actually be angry with his father for leaving; but since this parent is no longer in the home, the boy's hostility is directed toward the remaining parent.

A child's misbehavior often leads to punishment by Mother. Sometimes this alleviates feelings of guilt in the youngster. In other cases it makes the child feel that he has been rejected by both parents.

Besides exhibiting uncontrolled or antisocial behavior, a child may become sad or depressed. He may develop complaints such as headache, nausea, abdominal pain, poor appetite, and so forth. He may do poorly in school, not concentrate on his work, or refuse to go to school. A younger child, three to five years of age, who had been toilet trained may begin wetting the bed at night. Sleep disturbances or nightmares may occur. As a matter of fact, any of these, and other symptoms, may result from the youngster's feelings of insecurity when his home is broken up.

A child may also try to behave exceptionally well, fearing that, if he does not do so, he may have to leave just as his father did.

Parents who have been separated or divorced are often

understandably upset themselves. Nevertheless, they should realize that their children's misbehavior and other symptoms of physical or emotional distress may be related to anxiety regarding separation and a fear of being abandoned completely.

We should let a child know we understand that he may feel upset because his father has left the home. A mother could say to her son, "If I were a boy I would feel angry if my mother and father got a divorce." Even if he has been told before that the separation was in no way his fault or the fault of his siblings, this idea may have to be repeated to him.

When Jerry's mother threatened to send him back to his father, she was aggravating his fear of being abandoned. The younger the child, the greater his need to know that someone will take care of him. When his family is disrupted, he requires even more assurance that he can depend on the remaining parent.

Jerry's mother should have told him that he might be upset because of what happened to his family, and this might be why he was having trouble behaving in school. Rather than threatening to send him away, she should have asked him if he had any questions he wanted to ask her about what had occurred and what worries he had about himself.

Older teen-age children may present more of a problem. If a mother really cannot control them, it may be necessary for her to discuss the situation with her former husband. Occasionally a decision will be made to have an adolescent live with his father. Here, too, it would be best for the parents to decide the matter and then tell their offspring, rather than have the mother threaten such action because of her own frustration in dealing with him.

In a divorced family the child who now lives with one parent (usually the mother) will have concerns about who will care for him if anything happens to that parent. If the father is still interested in his child and is maintaining contact with him, the mother should specifically tell the youngster that his father will take care of him if anything happens to her.

As mentioned before, it is advisable for all parents of children under eighteen to give adequate thought to selecting the people who would care for their children were both parents to die. But this is especially important with children who have experienced the disrupting effects of separation and divorce. They should know what arrangements have been made for their future care should anything happen to both parents.

The Child and Sexual Impulses

Ten-year-old Eddie came over to his mother, hugged her tightly, and kissed her on the lips.

His mother enjoyed this but felt uncomfortable at the same time. "Why, Eddie," she said, "you kissed Mother like a little lover."

SUCH AN episode might happen in many families. Boys do feel attracted to their mothers; at times, they may demonstrate their affections in a rather passionate manner.

When there has been a divorce, a mother may be lonely and not as mindful as she should be of avoiding behavior that might be sexually stimulating to a child. Many children have sexual feelings toward their parents and are sometimes very uncomfortable because of such feelings. They sense that something is improper about this and that they need to be helped in controlling it.

While we should try to answer any questions about sex which are asked by our children, we should attempt to avoid behavior that will be sexually stimulating to them. In our culture, parents are wise not to parade around nude in front of their youngsters. They should also permit their children to have proper privacy.

After a separation or divorce, a mother may be so upset

that she almost looks for excuses to take her children into her bed to keep her company. No matter what the age of the child, this type of action should be avoided. Boys will find it pleasurable to snuggle up next to Mother in bed, but they may also have uncomfortable feelings about this. With Father out of the immediate picture, a son may feel guilty about taking his place.

At times fathers have custody of the children and the same type of situation occurs. Recently, I heard of a father who would lie down each evening with his young teen-age daughter. Of course, this is not the way things should be, and teen-age girls can be upset by lying down with their father all the time. This girl was upset about this and told her mother, who lived in another part of town. But she asked her mother not to say anything to her father because she feared he would be angry about it. This mother, under the circumstances, could only tell the child that she knew how she felt. The parent encouraged her to tell her father that she was uncomfortable about his lying down with her and ask him not to do so.

Some parents may be openly seductive with their youngsters. Others, who do not have much social life of their own, may be unaware that their actions can encourage their children's sexual fantasies.

When a boy kisses his mother in a way that makes her uncomfortable, as Eddie did, she should not get angry at him, but she should discourage such behavior. She should tell him simply, "This is not the way a boy kisses his mother." She can let him know she loves him as her son, but she is his mother and not a girl friend.

It is difficult to tell a parent exactly what is proper in terms of physical closeness and contact with a child. We can say that if a parent feels stimulated by, or uncomfortable with, a child's caresses it is important to set some limits. This can be done by being careful not to encourage this type of behavior, and by telling the child that this way of showing affection is not appropriate when it is with one's parent.

Mother's Confidante

Barbara, who was eleven years old, was concerned because her mother had been upset and unhappy since the divorce.

"You can tell me your troubles, Mother. I'll listen. Maybe it will help."

AFTER A divorce, mothers in particular may have problems with feelings of loneliness. They usually have custody of the children. Even if a mother works, she still has to look after her offspring.

She may be resentful of the fact that her former husband sees the children only one day a week, or less, and is free to do whatever he wants to do the rest of the time. Depending on the circumstances which led to the divorce, she may miss her husband and wish that things had been different.

Under these conditions of loneliness and resentment, she may turn to her children for comfort. A daughter may sense her mother's feelings of despair, as Barbara did. Assuming an adult-like pose, she will offer to be a listening post for Mother. In other instances, the mother may put the child in the position of a confidante who must listen to her troubles. The youngster's advice may be sought by the parent on matters which the child is not qualified to discuss. The relationship becomes like that of two girl friends, rather than mother and daughter.

The development of such a situation is not good for either parent or child. Following a divorce, a woman should realize that it is normal for her to feel lonely and perhaps angry. She may even undergo a process of mourning similar to the one which follows the death of a loved one. But she should also remember that her children may be experiencing some of these same feelings.

She should avoid leaning on her offspring, for this puts more responsibility on them than is justified. They are still children. They still have to proceed with their own emotional growth and development under less than ideal circumstances. It is unfair to place upon them the burden of trying to act more adult and more mature than their parents.

If a child offers to be Mother's confidante, what should one say to her? She can be told that Mother appreciates her understanding and concern. She should be told that it is normal for her mother to be unhappy because she is no longer married. But Mother will get over this eventually, and will find ways of working out her own problems.

Her mother can say it is likely that her daughter misses her father too, and is unhappy over the matter of the divorce. The divorce is in no way the child's fault, however. Her job is to go on with her daily activities, such as school, music lessons, clubs, and so forth, and Mother wants her to continue giving attention to these things.

In the family disrupted by divorce, another situation may occur, similar to what sometimes happens when a parent dies. The son of a divorced mother may say that, because his father is no longer in the home, he will be the man of the house. Sometimes his mother (or a well-meaning but misguided relative) will tell him, "Now you'll have to take care of Mother" or "You must be the man of the house now." If there is a teen-age son, his mother may sometimes unconsciously put him in the role of a substitute husband. A daughter, left in custody of her father, may take over the household by doing the cooking and cleaning. She may imagine she has taken her mother's place, and act as if she has done so.

Regardless of the age of the child, it is not healthy for him to be put in the position of taking an absent parent's place, or of even imagining he can do this. If a boy acts as if he is the man of the house, he should be told that he is still the son, even though his parents are divorced. He is not responsible for taking care of his mother. She will still take care of him if he is young enough to need care.

If Mother must work and a child has to be given additional responsibility for taking care of himself, the reasons for this should be explained. But it should be stressed that Mother and Father will continue to be the parents and the youngster will continue to be their child, rather than man or woman of the house.

Divorced Parent and the Grandparents

After her divorce, Mrs. Parker moved in with her mother and father. One evening her son, Gary, came to her complaining. "Grandma told me I had to go to bed now. You told me I could stay up until eight thirty. Who's the boss of me anyway?"

SOMETIMES A divorced woman (or man, if he has custody of the children) will move back into her parents' home. Financial conditions may dictate this. Or she may feel that it will be a help to have them care for the children if she goes back to work.

In any event, problems may be created for her and the youngsters. Depending on the personalities of the grandparents, much conflict may develop over questions of discipline for the children.

The children may already be upset because they have to adjust to the absence of their father. They may have lived through a time of much bickering and disagreement between their parents. Part of the argument may have centered around the handling of the children. More than other youngsters, they need stability and consistency in their lives.

Instead, they may be confronted with conflicting views on rules and discipline. Mother may tell them to do something one way, and Grandmother may order them to do it differently. Perhaps the grandparents resent the additional burden of the children. Because of the divorce they may feel that their daughter has been a failure or has disgraced them. This may lead them to be unjustifiably hard on their grandchildren. Or they may feel sorry for the "poor kids" and give in to their wishes too much, negating efforts of the mother who is trying to maintain consistent limits.

In other instances the mother may take advantage of her parents, and behave as if she were an adolescent again, free of responsibilities. She may become involved in dating and in recreational activities, essentially abdicating her role as Mother.

A woman who is divorced should give considerable thought to the question of whether or not to move in with her parents. Sometimes, compelling practical considerations determine her decision, but at other times it may simply seem the most convenient and easiest course to take. She should be aware that the existence of multiple authorities in a household can be very confusing to children.

If such a living arrangement is necessary, an attempt should be made firmly to establish the fact that there is one set of rules. The child should be told that Mother makes the rules and Grandmother and Grandfather help to see that they are carried out. When there is disagreement between the parent and grandparents, a compromise should be worked out when the children are not around. When a decision is reached, the youngsters should be informed as to what will be expected of them. It should be presented to them as Mother's idea with the grandparents in agreement.

Divorced mothers, or fathers, holding down a job and having custody of the children, may have to employ a housekeeper or baby-sitter. The children should be told that since the parent must work they will be left in the care of the sitter.

The parent should also tell them that the caretaker will expect them to follow the rules set down by Mother. If they feel the rules are unfair or they are being mistreated in any way, they can discuss it with Mother. She will then correct the situation if she feels that anything should be changed.

CHAPTER VIII

Remarriage

The Angry Stepchild

"You're not my mother," the little girl said. *"I hate you and you can't tell me what to do."*

"You ungrateful kid," her stepmother answered. *"After all that I try to do for you."*

NOT EVERY stepchild will actually say the words that this little girl did, but virtually all of them at times will harbor similar feeings. Not many stepmothers will respond in the way that this mother did, but most could experience such a reaction to the anger of their stepchild.

Stepparents usually try hard to be good parents. They rarely fit the picture of the mean stepmothers in the fairy tales. Yet, despite all the efforts they make, at some point their stepchild may express his or her anger, and this outburst may be the result of some minor request that has been made by the parent.

All children sometimes have hateful feelings toward their parents. If we are going to do an adequate job as parents, it is necessary for us at times to be an agent of frustration in the life of our child. When not given his way, the child will likely become angry. He needs permission for his feelings, but he needs to learn that he must control his actions and be responsible for these actions.

While the handling of anger may be a fact of life for all children and parents, the circumstances become more complex for stepparents and their stepchildren. The child of his natural parents may say, "You're not my parents or you wouldn't treat me this way," but the parents have no conflict about the reality of their having produced this offspring.

However, the stepparent who is endeavoring to be a good mother or good father and then hears the words "You're not my mother" or "You're not my father" does not have immediately available the reassurance of the natural parent's reality. The child becomes angry and arouses the counter-anger of the stepparent. How the parent responds can determine whether this episode will represent the onset of a worsening relationship, or whether it will be a step in the evolvement of a better relationship between the people involved.

The stepmother should be aware of her own anger but hopefully exercise some control in the way she responds to the child's outburst. She should remember that it is common for children to be angry when frustrated, and that her stepchild may have mixed feelings to deal with. If his natural mother has died, the child may have wished for a substitute mother but still have negative feelings about someone taking his mother's place. Where a divorce has occurred, the child usually still has contact with his natural mother or father, and he may have to contend with the question of divided loyalties.

What could the stepmother say and do in the scene depicted? She could say to the child, "That's right. I'm not the mother from whom you were born, but I am acting as a mother to you now and I will continue to do so. You can feel as angry as you want to feel. I remember when I was angry with my mother. If you don't like what I tell you to do, you can give me your opinion about it, but if I still feel that my request was reasonable you'll have to do it. I know that you feel angry like most children do and that's O.K., but you still have to do what I say."

The words, of course, may be different, but it is important to let the child know that, while you are not usurping her parent's place, you will function as a parent, and you will accept the fact that she can be angry with you as she would be with her natural parent. You should try to make the child aware of the fact that it is not abnormal to be angry, and that one need not fear that angry feelings or wishes will physically hurt anyone.

When a child combines his feelings with destructive action,

it is important to let him know that the feelings are permissible but the action is not, and it is the action that must be controlled.

Being a Parent

"Jeff didn't do his chores today," said the boy's stepfather to his wife.
"Why didn't you make him do them?" she asked.
"Since he's your child, you tell him what to do. I don't want him to be angry with me about this," her husband answered.

THE STEPFATHER who made this statement was an excellent father to Jeff and his siblings in many ways. He liked them and devoted time to doing things with them that they all enjoyed. But he also had a mistaken notion that, since he was not their biological father, he should leave the discipline to their mother.

He was uncomfortable with the prospect of the children disliking him if he were to discipline them in any way. Fortunately, he was able to change his attitude. He was assured that the children could tolerate and accept his disciplinary measures because he was also showing in so many other ways that he cared for them.

A stepparent should assume the role of a parent in the household. In the eyes of his stepchildren, he should not be merely the husband of their mother. Ideally he should become a substitute father. If the children's father is dead, the stepfather need not take his place in their affections; but he can make a contribution to the youngsters' development by acting as their father. If their father is absent because of divorce, the stepfather should still function as the head of the household where the children are residing the majority of the time.

As with any father, the children will dislike him if his main function is to punish them. If he is also interested in them and their activities, however, they may grumble, but they will accept his discipline. It is much better for a good stepfather to let the children know that he and the mother agree on discipline.

Sometimes, when the children's natural mother remarries she may expect the stepfather to love her children as much as she does. She may be upset if she feels that he is not being as "good" to them as he is to his own children of a previous marriage. Generally this is not a reasonable expectation.

If a stepparent is trying to be fair, firm, and kind to the children, his behavior should be appreciated. His feelings are not apt to be as strong toward his stepchildren as toward his own. He can still be a good father-figure without having to love all his children equally. But he will not be a good substitute father if he is not willing to accept both the giving and disciplining aspects of his role.

Some stepmothers feel threatened by the memory of their predecessors. When she marries a widower with children, a woman may immediately come into a home and completely redecorate the place so that it will now be "hers." The youngsters may have bad feelings about this activity, thinking that their stepmother is trying to get rid of the memory of their mother. It is understandable for a woman to want her home decorated according to her taste, but it would be much better to go about doing this in a gradual manner. When the children get to know her and relate to her, they will not feel as upset about changes she will make as they might if she begins to make changes as soon as she moves in.

Stepparents may try very hard and the children still seem unappreciative or hostile. Parents should remember that the children have a lot of conflicts to resolve. Many stepchildren give their stepparents an awfully hard time, then look back when they are older and realize how much benefit was derived because the stepparent was willing to function as a genuine parent.

Deciding To Remarry

Mrs. Sanford has been divorced for two years. Six months ago she met a man to whom she has become quite attached. She is seriously thinking of marrying him. One evening she spoke to her children and said, "You know I like Steve very much. Do you want me to marry him?"

WHEN A widowed or divorced person is contemplating remarriage, the welfare of any children involved should be considered strongly. Nevertheless, the decision of whether or not to marry should not be left up to the children.

Mrs. Sanford may honestly have felt that she would not remarry if her children did not approve. But it is wrong to let children believe they can be responsible for such a decision.

Sometimes, however, a mother may pay little attention to the question of how her youngsters will fit in after she remarries. She may feel that if her future husband loves her enough, he will love her children too. She may let herself believe this even if he tells her he is not particularly fond of children.

A parent, especially the one who has custody of children, should pay a great deal of attention to the attitudes about children that are expressed by the intended partner verbally or by his behavior. Even the stepparent who genuinely loves children will be confronted with problems. Youngsters have mixed feelings about the remarriage of their parent. If the other parent is living and unmarried, the children may still be wishing for the reunion of their parents. The offspring of a dead parent may feel it is disloyal for the surviving parent to marry again.

An eighteen-year-old college girl who was dating regularly

herself became very upset when her father began to go out with women. He had been a widower for three years. A twelve-year-old boy stuck close to his father, even developing a school phobia so that he could remain at home and be able to keep in touch with Dad regularly. After his mother's death he was fearful of something happening to his father, but he also wanted to make sure that his father was not going out with a female companion.

A parent whose spouse has died may find her children objecting to her going out on dates. She should ask them why they do not want her to go. The youngsters may then voice their objections. In some instances children, especially the younger ones, may not want to state their reasons.

In either case, the mother should tell them that she knows they miss their father, as she does, and she understands that they may not like the idea of her going out with other men. However, Father is dead and he cannot return, and she and the children must continue to live their lives. She can tell them this is what their father would have wanted them to do. She can assure them that she loves them very much, but it is important for her to meet men so that she might find someone she will like enough to marry. She can also say that, if she had died and Father had lived, she would have wanted him to find another wife.

In a situation where the parent is divorced and the children object to her dating, they should be told that Mother and Father are no longer married to each other and will not be remarried. The children may wish that the parents would get back together, but this is not going to happen. The youngsters should be told that, while their feelings are understood by the parents, each parent has the right to do what he or she wants in regard to social life.

When a relationship develops to the point where marriage is contemplated, the parent should not ask for her children's permission. She must take their welfare into consideration in making up her mind, but the responsibility for the decision must be hers. If she feels she has found someone she likes, and who basically will be kind and fair to her children, she should tell the children. She can say that she has found someone who she feels will be a good husband to her and a substitute father for them. If they have objections she should let them voice these, but the decision must be hers.

Competition with Stepparent

Tony's mother had been remarried for two months. His father died several years ago. Tony liked his stepfather at first but lately seemed to resent him. One afternoon his mother saw Tony looking tearful.

"What's the trouble?" she asked.

"You love him more than you do me, don't you?" cried Tony.

TONY, WHO was eight years old, had mixed feelings about his mother's remarriage. He did miss having a father. His stepfather was nice to him before the marriage and continued to treat him well afterward. But having had his mother's attention all to himself for a long time, the boy was finding it difficult to share her with another male.

All children may have competitive feelings toward the parent of the same sex. The offspring of a divorced or widowed parent will have lived with only one parent for a period of time. A mother may have fostered a close attachment with her son because of her own loneliness in the absence of a husband.

As in Tony's case, a boy may show jealousy of his stepfather whom he sees as a new competitor. A girl may feel the same way toward her stepmother. Parents should recognize the possibility of such feelings being present in their youngster.

When a child says, "You love him more than you do me," a parent may think, "Now isn't that cute." She might react by teasing the child. She may say, "Tony! don't tell me you're jealous." The child, hearing this, may feel embarrassed and angry. He is feeling something strongly and his mother is making fun of him. Another mother may say, "Now isn't that silly?" The child does not think his ideas are silly. Or a mother may say, "That's childish. You shouldn't feel that way." He is being told that there is something wrong with being a child and that his feelings may not be normal. Parents who answer in ways similar to these do not intend to make things worse, but there is a good chance that they are doing so.

How should we deal with this situation? What shall we tell the child who, by what he says or by the way he acts, indicates his concern about Mother's love for him? He should not be teased, or shamed, or made to feel that he is expressing an abnormal emotion.

He should be told that we understand how he feels, and that any boy or girl could have the same feelings under similar conditions. We can tell him that it must be difficult, at first, to share some of his mother's attention with a new father, even though he himself is also getting attention from the stepfather. A mother can also tell her son that she loves him as much as she always has, that no one can ever take his place as her *son*.

She should tell him that the kind of feeling a wife has for a husband is different from the love a mother and father have for a child. She can tell him that, even though it may be hard for him to understand this now, he will know what she means as he grows older. But, for now, he will have to believe her when she says that she loves his stepfather differently from the way she loves him, but not any more than she loves him.

It is also important to remember that, to a certain degree, the kindest, most understanding stepparent will be seen by the child as an interloper. A child may not express this directly but may show it in his behavior and attitudes. The wise stepparent will try to recognize this. If he can let the youngster know that he is aware of the feeling and is neither threatened nor angered by it, he will enable the child to work out his problems.

The stepfather could say to his stepson, "I bet most boys feel jealous when Mother gets married. You must feel that way sometimes." The boy may or may not comment on this, but just hearing a statement like this, delivered by his stepfather without anger, could be extremely helpful to a child.

Half-Siblings

Mr. Russell had been awarded custody of his daughter, Lynn, because her mother had a mental illness which required hospitalization. He had remarried and now had another daughter. Lynn was now six years old and her half-sister, Julie, was three and a half.

Lynn's mother recovered and Lynn would now go out on visits with her mother each Saturday. She would often come back with a present which her mother had bought for her.

On one occasion Julie said to her mother, "I wish I had two mommys like Lynn so I could go out and get presents too."

BOTH CHILDREN in this family had problems. The older daughter, Lynn, had suffered some emotional deprivation because of her mother's illness and subsequent absence from the home. Now she had to deal with the confusion of having two mother figures. She knew that she had been born of her natural mother, but the one who took care of her each day was her stepmother. Her father felt sorry for her because of what she had been through in her young life, and he tended to pay more attention to her than to his younger daughter.

As far as the matter of two mothers was concerned, there is not much she can be told, other than the fact that both mothers are interested in her and like her. In the long run, her picture of what a mother is will likely be a composite based on both her mother's and stepmother's characteristics.

Julie, the younger half-sister, began to have a problem in that she felt she was missing something. She would see her older sister go out on visits with her mother and come back with toys and other presents. She also noticed that Father was paying more attention to Lynn than he was to her.

The parents in such a situation should be aware of what is happening. It is understandable that they would be concerned with the difficulties of the older child, but they should not forget the needs and feelings of the younger half-sibling. This may be similar to the case where much attention is paid to a handicapped youngster while his healthy siblings may be neglected.

In the family described here, we should recognize that the younger child may be upset and subsequently resentful because of what she sees as favored treatment for the older sister. We would usually tend to think of the older daughter as deprived since she is not living with her natural mother and the younger one is. The young child will not see things in this light, however. She will only know that her sister is getting presents and attention while she is not.

It would be well in such circumstances to ask the older child's mother not to buy presents on each visiting day. When something is bought for her daughter, a small gift could be sent home with her to be given to the younger sibling. With any two children, we cannot see to it that they are treated exactly equal. But we should try to control factors that would make one child feel she is getting much less attention than her sibling.

Children's Need for Stability

Jennifer, who was eight, and her six-year-old brother, Henry, had lived with their mother and stepfather for the past two years. Before their parents' divorce the household had been in a turmoil with much bickering and unrest. Their present home had a calmer atmosphere, and the children had settled into a fairly good routine.

Their father, who lived in another city, had remarried about nine months before and wanted them to come for Christmas. The children wanted to remain in their present home on Christmas Day. Their father called his former wife and said, "I don't care if the kids are upset. They'll get over it. It's our turn to have them for Christmas. I told them to come and I want you to send them up here."

ON CHRISTMAS, or on other special occasions, both sets of parents want their children with them. If the children are getting along fairly well in their physical and emotional development, there should be some amicable arrangement for holidays to be shared with each set of parents on alternate years.

Youngsters who have lived through the divorce of their parents and the breaking up of the home need a period of stability, however. In the situation described above, Jennifer and her brother were still getting over the disruptive effects of their parents' separation and divorce. In these circumstances it was very unfair of their father to insist on his rights. Besides being inconsiderate of the feelings and well-being of his offspring, he is following a shortsighted course if he really wants to have a good relationship with his children.

In effect, this father was blaming his former wife for his

children's not wanting to be in his home on Christmas. He was wrong; it was the children's wish to remain at home during the holiday. At their age, the recently established stability was important, and being home on Christmas Day was part of this.

Had this father been able to exercise better judgment, he would not have insisted that the children come to visit him. He could have told them he understood that being home on Christmas was very important to them. He could have said that, even though he would miss being with them, he hoped they would have a good holiday, and he would be looking forward to seeing them as soon as he could.

Parents sometimes insist on their rights because they want the children to know they are interested in them. But the most genuine interest is that which makes the children's welfare the primary consideration. This should take precedence over the parents' feelings or wishes.

We should remember that the children's need for stability in their lives is more important than the convenience of the parents. Youngsters who have lived through unsettling periods may not want to leave home to visit the other parent. In such an instance, it would be advisable for the parent to visit them if he is interested in maintaining contact with his children.

If the two sets of parents cannot settle questions of visits without involving the children in continued or renewed bickering, they should at least seek the advice of a neutral counselor in order to work out a pattern of functioning that will be in the best interest of their children.

CHAPTER IX

Sex

Elementary Sex Education

"How does the baby get into the mommy's tummy?" asked the three-year-old.
"The daddy puts it there," replied his mother.
"How does he put it there?"
"Go ask your father."
He went to his father and said, "Mommy said the daddy puts the baby in the mommy's tummy. How does he get it in there? Does he push it in?"

THE FIRST thought that came to mind when this father heard the boy's question was, "Has he seen us having intercourse?" However, when he asked what the boy meant by "Does he push it in?" he learned that his youngster was imagining a fully grown baby, somehow taken by the father and pushed into the mother's abdomen.

Much controversy still surrounds sex education. Should the subject be taught in schools? If it is taught, by whom and in what manner? And so on. But few would dispute the fact that, ideally, sex education should be an ongoing process in a home from the time an infant is born.

What we teach children in relation to the morality of sexual functioning depends on our own background, our religious beliefs, and in general what we think is proper or improper, advantageous or not advantageous. And on what we consider a healthy or unhealthy attitude in sexual matters. No one can dictate our teachings in regard to this important aspect of life. We should make up our minds as to what we think is right and then impart our views of things to our children. When our children are older, they will develop their own standards of behavior, which could be quite different from our own.

Insofar as basic information about the anatomy and simple

physiological principles of sexual functioning is concerned, we should be prepared to answer the questions our children bring to us at the time that they bring them. If we know how an internal-combustion engine works and our child asks us a question about it, we answer him readily. Yet, if he asks, "Where do babies come from?" or "How are babies made?" we often hem and haw. Obviously, our own upbringing and past experience affect our reaction, but we should overcome our reticence and supply ourselves with the basic knowledge with which we can answer our offspring's questions.

Having certain facts in mind is an aid when replying to a youngster's query. If a parent answers questions honestly to a child at any age, it is likely that the child will feel comfortable about asking more questions later. At times, even after we have given a good explanation, children will return at a later date and ask the same questions, either to reassure themselves about the answer or because they really had not understood us the first time.

The child's sex education, as far as the essential facts are concerned, very likely will begin with curiosity about the anatomical differences between himself and a sister, or other female infants or children whom he has seen in the nude. He should be told that boys and girls are born different. A boy has a penis and testicles, and a girl does not. Boys grow up to be men and can become fathers. Girls grow up to be women and can become mothers. Although girls do not have a penis, they do have a small space in the same area with two openings, one of which is a small opening through which they urinate.

Children often think that, because a girl has to sit down to urinate, the urine comes from her rectum, and they often imagine that this is where the baby comes out of the mother. If a very young child asks where babies come from, he should be told that they grow in the mother's abdomen in a special place, but not in the same place where her food goes. At times this is all they initially want to know.

When the youngster asks how the baby gets inside the

mother, he should be told that it starts from a tiny egg which is about the size of a pencil dot, and that this egg comes from inside the mother's abdomen. In order to begin growing, this egg has to be joined by a much tinier sperm which comes from the father. Too often, children are told about a seed from the father, and they may develop various erroneous ideas about how the seed is planted.

A child may listen to the explanation and not ask anything more at this point about the egg and the sperm. If he does ask how the sperm gets into the mother, however, we should tell him simply and directly. We can say that nature has made people so that the father's penis fits into a special space in the mother which is called a vagina, and this place is located in front between the mother's legs. The sperm goes from the father's penis into the mother's vagina and then joins up with the egg. The egg then begins to grow and develops into a baby which grows inside the mother in the uterus (or womb) for nine months.

Children often wonder how the baby gets out of the mother. They can develop all sorts of strange theories to explain how this happens. When they ask, they should be answered in a forthright manner. We can tell them that it might be hard for them to believe how it happens, but when a mother goes to the hospital to have a baby, a special place opens up in her body between her legs. The skin and muscles stretch and there is enough room for the baby to squeeze through, usually with the head coming first. The doctor helps the baby in getting out. After the baby is born, the mother's stretched skin and muscles go back to the way they were before. If a child asks what helps the baby out, he can be told that there are muscles in the mother's uterus that push down so that the baby comes out.

Youngsters may want to know how the baby gets fed and breathes inside the mother. It can be explained that things are different from the way they will be after the baby is born. Inside the mother a special tube attaches to the baby's belly, through which the infant gets the things he needs to grow.

When the baby is born he doesn't need this tube anymore, and all that is left will be his belly button. Once he is born he breathes air through his lungs and his food goes to his stomach.

If children are given facts about sex in a straightforward manner, they will accept them as the matter-of-fact information they should be. Later, of course, they will want to know more and should be answered accordingly, or we can tell them that we will get books for them that will help to answer their questions.

Occasionally, children may come into a room while their parents are having sexual relations. Very young children may misinterpret what they see and may believe that the father is in some way hurting the mother. If we are aware that a child has been in the room, we should try to find out what he thought was happening and correct his misconceptions. For example, if a child believes that his father was hurting his mother, he should be assured by both parents that this was not the case. He can be told that his mother and father love each other and were doing something that grown-up men and women do together. We can also tell him that not only were they not hurting one another, but that they were both getting pleasure from what they were doing.

The foregoing is concerned mainly with imparting factual information. But it should be emphasized that our child's attitudes toward sex will be dependent on what we teach him about our standards and beliefs, and even more, on what he observes of our behavior.

Adolescent Development

Julia's mother was talking to the pediatrician. "You know, Doctor, that Julia is only nine and a half years old. Her breasts are developing and she'll probably be menstruating soon. Is this normal?"

WITH THE onset of adolescence, chronological age ceases to be of much use in comparing children to one another. Some girls may begin to menstruate at nine or ten years of age, while others may not start until they are sixteen or seventeen.

Girls who find themselves at either end of this spectrum will be concerned about it. Parents should be aware that the child may be embarrassed when she has to undress in front of her peers in a gym class or camp situation. The youngster may be an object of curiosity or she may be teased by her acquaintances.

They should be told that, while most girls experience their first menstrual period at the age of twelve or thirteen, some may be several years younger or older when it occurs. In either case, the child should be assured that she is perfectly normal if, among her group of friends, she is one of the first or one of the last to begin menstruating.

Frequently, a girl's periods do not occur regularly when she first begins to menstruate. Some children become very concerned about this. A few may fear pregnancy even though they have not had intercourse. They have heard that if you miss a period you may be pregnant. Girls should be told that it is not unusual to miss periods when you first start menstruating and you cannot be pregnant if you have not had sexual intercourse.

Children should know what menstruation is. It should be explained to them that, during adolescence, when a girl's body begins to develop, changes occur internally as well as externally. The outward signs of change are the development of breasts, changes in the shape of the hips, and the growth of pubic hair and hair under the arms. Inside the girl's body the ovaries will soon become capable of discharging an egg once a month. By means of substances called hormones that exist in a person's body, nature acts in such a way as to prepare the lining of the uterus so that, if an egg is fertilized by a sperm, it can grow and develop. When the egg is not joined by a sperm, the prepared lining of the uterus is not needed, and parts of it become detached and leave the uterus through the vagina. The discharge from the vagina contains blood and cells from the lining of the uterus. The menstrual period usually lasts about four days, but it may last a week. A girl should be assured that the amount of blood she loses will not be harmful to her.

Boys too can have problems related to the age that changes begin to occur in their bodies. When most boys are twelve to fourteen years of age their scrotum and testicles begin to enlarge, and after this the penis also increases in size. They also have a growth of pubic hair, followed by a growth of hair in the armpit, and then facial hair. Their voices change.

About one year after the beginning of these changes, they usually have acquired the capacity to produce sperm, and they may have nocturnal emissions ("wet dreams"). During sleep there may be a discharge of semen, a fluid which contains the sperm. A boy may or may not have a sex dream along with the emission. Boys should be told there is no danger of their losing too many sperm cells even if they have frequent dreams of this kind. Boys should also be assured that there is nothing wrong with them if they have not had wet dreams.

The boy who develops late will be very conscious of the fact that his penis and scrotum are smaller than the other boys with whom he has to dress in the locker room. Fathers should be aware that a son may feel this way even though he says nothing about it. The youngster should be told that it is normal for some boys to develop later than others. He should be told that a boy may feel uncomfortable if he is less physically mature than other boys his age. He should be assured that, in time, his sexual organs will be more developed and that there is nothing wrong with him. Some boys undergo the changes of puberty as early as ten or eleven years, and they have to be told that they are perfectly normal even though their friends have not as yet undergone these changes.

While masturbation is no longer thought of as causing

insanity and other illnesses, many children still feel guilty about this. Parents occasionally will not say anything directly to the adolescents about masturbation but will be critical if the youngsters stay in their rooms with the doors closed or if they are spending too much time in the bathroom. Teen-agers should be given the idea that masturbation is not harmful and it is not wrong to have sexual daydreams while they are masturbating. The parent who believes that an adolescent is masturbating excessively should look upon this behavior as a result of unhappiness in the child's life, rather than the cause of trouble. One should then consider what is going on in the life of the child in general, and not just in the area of sexual impulses.

One common occurrence which causes many adolescent boys to worry is the enlargement of their breasts. Usually both breasts enlarge, but there may be a difference in size on the two sides; at times, only one breast is involved. The enlargement of breast tissue is influenced by the increased secretion of hormones.

The breasts will decrease in size. This may happen within a few months or it may take a year or two. Boys should be told that there is nothing wrong with them, and that this breast enlargement is not abnormal and will not persist. They should also be told that it occurs frequently and that, usually, no treatment is necessary for this condition.

The New Sexual Freedom

Jane, a high school senior, went to see her family doctor for her yearly physical examination. The physician found that she was in good health, but she looked troubled.

"Is there anything special bothering you today, Jane?" he asked.

Somewhat hesitantly she said, "Doctor, so many of the girls at school are talking about taking the 'pill' and 'going all the way.' Is there anything wrong with me because I'm not doing it?"

SEX IS very much with us these days. Everywhere we turn, we are confronted by it. The pendulum has swung from a time when no one talked about sex to an age when there seems nothing else to talk about.

We are reminded of sex in double-meaning television commercials. It is brought to our attention in the battles between opponents and proponents of sex education in the schools. The communication media are supplying a tremendous amount of information about this once-forbidden subject.

Certainly, I would feel that the situation was a healthier one when sex was openly discussed instead of avoided, as once was the case in most households. Children should feel that if they want to talk to each other and to their parents about sex, they can do so. But today, in seeing young children and adolescents the physician becomes aware of many instances in which ignorance of physical matters relating to sex has been replaced by confusion relating to the subject in its many social and psychological aspects.

Fortunately, books offering home medical advice no longer contain the statement that masturbation leads to insanity. Most parents accept, at least intellectually, the fact that masturbation is an almost universal phenomenon among boys and very frequent among girls. Nowadays we may find material in books stating that every boy has tried to suck his own penis at some time or other. Such statements may cause undue anxiety in children and their parents. They may even feel that something is wrong if these things have not been attempted. Children should not be punished for sexual experimentation, but neither should we feel, or make the child feel, that he is abnormal because he has not tried "everything in the book."

The increased public acceptance and discussion of sex has given young people more freedom in this sphere. Theoretically, at least, the advent of the "pill" has freed young women from the fear of pregnancy and allowed for some relaxation of the double standard regarding sexual conduct. ("It's all right for him but not for her.") At times, however, this double standard appears to be very much with us still. For example, a college boy may be living with a nice girl who cooks for him, sleeps with him, is faithful to him, and in general takes good care of him. This same young man may strongly advise his sister, who has just started college, to remain a virgin until she gets married.

But many young people may be adversely affected by the increased frankness in our culture relative to sexual matters. Many children, like Jane in our opening illustration, begin to wonder if there is anything wrong with them because they do not want, or are not ready, to engage in sexual relations. Whereas in previous generations a girl was made to feel "damned if she did" by her peers, she may now be made to feel "damned if she doesn't."

More so than in former times, young males may begin to doubt their own manliness because they have not yet had intercourse when "everybody else is doing it." We need to let them know that there are differing feelings about sex: there are various standards of behavior by which each of us decides to live; there are quantitative differences in the sexual needs of individuals just as there are in relation to food; and others have a right to do as they please without in any way making our own decision wrong.

What should we say to a girl who brings us a question such as the one that Jane brought to her doctor? We can tell her not to believe everything she hears. Some girls today won't admit to being virgins because it implies that they "are not with it." She can be told that it is normal for a girl her age to have sexual urges and curiosity about these feelings. But she should know that she is not abnormal if she does not feel it is right for her to engage in intercourse, or if she feels she is not ready for such activity.

One of the problems of the so-called sexual revolution is that, while varying degrees of knowledge have been imparted to children and there has been increasing sexual activity, there has been a lack of teaching about the responsibility involved in sexual behavior. If we are doing our job as parents, we try to make our youngsters aware of the responsibilities and dangers of driving a car. Is there any reason why we should not try equally as hard to familiarize them with the obligations related to sexual functioning?

The number of cases of gonorrhea and syphilis in young people is rising markedly. In spite of the availability of contraceptive measures, unwanted pregnancies are also increasing. Adolescents are often unaware of the dangers involved in their sexual behavior. Often they are unmindful of, or unfamiliar with, the measures they should take to avoid pregnancy and disease. Young people should be told that a girl who is taking the "pill" or using contraceptive jelly or foam or a diaphragm may not get pregnant, but she can still catch a venereal disease or transmit it. The use of a rubber condom is not only a contraceptive method, but also serves to help prevent infection.

At the present time, given the state of our sexual mores, much confusion exists among young people. Standards of behavior vary in each generation, but parents still need to impart a set of values to their offspring. Whether the youngsters accept or reject their parents' way of looking at things will depend on many factors. One of the most important of these will be the child's feelings about his parents and their relationship to him in general. But, no matter what we teach our children in regard to sexual behavior, it is of extreme importance for them to exercise responsibility in what they are doing.

The question often arises, "Should the 'pill' be prescribed for teen-agers?" This is considered here, not from the standpoint of the possible medical dangers of contraceptive medication, but from the viewpoint of whether it is good or bad to sanction the use of the "pill" or prescribe it for unmarried adolescents.

If a teen-age or college-age girl comes to her parents and asks for the "pill," what should they say? Of course, there is no stock answer to this question. There is no formula to be used in dealing with this problem. But how should we approach such a situation?

My recommendation would be that the parent should not react with shock, horror, or anger. Neither should he answer with an automatic "Absolutely not" or an instantaneous "Yes." First, he should attempt to find out what the young lady may be trying to say. Is she trying to find out what her parents think about her having premarital intercourse? Is she looking for support of her own feelings of not really wanting to do what some of her acquaintances are doing? Or has she decided that, since this is something she is doing or plans to do, she wants to be responsible enough about her own behavior to prevent a pregnancy?

Adolescent girls certainly can be advised to keep their options about sexual behavior open. Their decisions about sex should be based on their own individual convictions, and not on what the crowd is doing. If a daughter seems to be asking for limits, her parents should let her know that they understand her dilemma and tell her that she should not feel abnormal if she doesn't do what some of her friends are doing. Doing what she herself feels is the right thing may be more worthwhile to her than superficial popularity. They can then tell her that they do not think it is advisable for her to take the "pill," and that she might postpone any decision about sexual intercourse until she makes up her own mind.

However, if a girl lets her parents know that she will be engaging in sexual relations, it would be wrong for her parents flatly to prohibit her from going to a physician for a discussion of the pros and cons of contraceptives of various kinds; and, hopefully, for some discussion of the meanings of her own decisions and behavior. It is far better to provide a sexually active child with proper contraceptive and medical advice than to have her subjected to an unwanted pregnancy and abortion.

While the liberalization of abortion laws is on balance a good thing, in some ways society has gone from illegal abortions to legalized ones without, at times, providing for advice and counsel for the affected young people. In some jurisdictions a letter from a psychiatrist is required before an abortion can be performed, testifying to the dangers of the pregnancy for the mother's mental health, but rarely is any meaningful therapy or discussion carried out with the patient. There may be no attempt to determine what factors produced the pregnancy in the first place, and often no contraceptive advice is provided afterward.

One of the most disheartening aspects of the current attitude toward sexual behavior is that sex seems to be becoming increasingly separated from intimacy. What was once in the realm of private pleasure has entered the area of public performance. We do not know what the eventual consensus will be relative to the sexual conduct of human beings. We can hope, however, that whether sex is premarital or marital, the involved partners will have regard for each other as people and not as objects. And if the opportunity presents itself, we should say this to our children.

Homosexuality

"Why do you always want to play the piano and listen to music?" one father asked his son. "Even if you are a little clumsy, why don't you go out and play ball with the boys? Do you want them to think you're a sissy?"

220   What Shall We Tell the Kids?

OPINIONS DIFFER regarding the homosexual way of life, varying from the belief that homosexuality is as normal as heterosexuality to the view that homosexuality is completely abnormal, and the homosexual person is either ill or a criminal.

We have no definitive answer to the question of why some individuals choose, or must adopt, a homosexual orientation. Many factors enter into this situation: the constitutional makeup of the individual, the personalities of his parents, his environment, and the various ways he experiences things as he is growing up.

With all the conflicting theories we hear about homosexuality, what should parents do in this regard concerning their own children?

Regardless of whether we consider homosexuality normal or abnormal, most of us would agree that it is easier to function in society as a heterosexual. Of course, if one accepts the viewpoint that certain children are born to be homosexuals, nothing much can be done about it. But, from a practical standpoint, as parents of young children we should adopt the attitude that elements within our control may be of importance in influencing sexual identity.

We do not want to approach a child in the manner of the father quoted above. He suggests that there is something wrong with a boy who enjoys playing the piano and music. He calls attention to awkwardness, something a child cannot control. He essentially tells his son that he cannot be considered masculine because he's not out playing ball. What kind of self-esteem can this youngster have when he hears all this from his father? And it is safe to assume that his dad's displeasure at not having an All-American boy is also communicated in many other ways.

A boy who is physically awkward is at a decided disadvantage in our culture with its emphasis on sports, particularly competitive athletics. Such a child can easily grow up feeling unmanly. As parents we can recognize our disappointment if our child lacks physical coordination. But we should make every effort to let him know that we like him for what he is.

A nonathletic youngster needs the support and approval of his father much more than the one who can go out and easily mix-it-up with the other boys. Even the frail, clumsy child will become more sure of himself and will develop more interest in athletic activities if his father has the understanding and patience to spend time giving him the necessary practice and encouragement. This is the important thing to do, rather than shaming a boy for his legitimate interests, whether they be art, music, or in some instances, cooking. If the latter, we might even inform him that chefs can earn an excellent living if they master their art, and the most famous chefs are men.

Just as a son benefits from his father's interest, a daughter should have the opportunity to be with her mother and to learn from her. Girls may, at times, demonstrate tomboyish behavior. Too much should not be made of this, and they should not be teased. Most girls discard this behavior during adolescence, if these tendencies are not reinforced by other personality problems.

In any event, it is not good for children to see that one parent is completely dominant and the other practically always submissive. Boys and girls need to experience warmth and affection from both parents. Because of a fear of homosexuality, many fathers seem afraid to express these sentiments toward their sons. When a boy is about six years of age, some fathers abruptly stop hugging or kissing him, as if there were a law against it. Children can be very confused by this behavior, and may interpret it as meaning the father no longer likes them. When a father is secure in terms of his own masculinity, he will not harm his son by being demonstrative with him.

There are parents who, prior to the birth of a child, make up their minds that the baby will be of a particular gender. Blue furniture and blue clothes may be purchased, as if the prospective infant cannot turn out to be a female. If a girl is born there may be tremendous discontent. The parent makes his disappointment known not only to friends and relatives, but also to his daughter as she is growing up, with statements such as, "We were really hoping for a boy when you came." Or the child may hear her father say, "This was supposed to be our little quarterback." Right from the beginning the girl may react to this by believing that there is something wrong with being feminine, and this can cause confusion in relation to her feminine identification. The same may be true for boys whose mother's disappointment is shown in a tendency in the early years to dress them in such a way that they are mistaken for little girls. Parents should keep in mind that their children's later sexual behavior can be affected by these early events.

When our youngsters reach adolescence, we must remember that they are not going to turn out to be homosexuals because they have some mutual sexual experiences with peers of the same sex. If this were true, and it is not, there would be many more homosexuals. If it comes to our attention that our children have engaged in some homosexual activity, we should not tell them they have done a terrible thing. We can honestly tell them that many teenagers try these things on occasion and it does not mean that they are abnormal or "queer."

Some children are naturally shy and, consequently, they are reluctant to pursue members of the opposite sex. Such behavior is not an indication that a boy will become a homosexual male or the girl a lesbian. We can reassure our child and let him know that many of us felt the same way in our adolescence. So many young people labor under the mistaken notion that they are the only ones who have these uncomfortable feelings when it comes to making any overture to a member of the opposite sex.

There will be adolescents who are having problems because they are homosexuals. Given the climate of opinion existing in our society, great anguish is not uncommon in a youngster who finds himself in this position. Usually he will keep his troubles from his parents. Often there will be indications which the parents do not notice, or do not choose to notice. Parents will be tremendously upset if they think their child is a homosexual. Thus, the homosexual child is very much in need of their understanding. They should not tell him that he is "awful" or that he has disgraced them and the family.

Homosexuality is either a condition that one is born with or one which results from psychological or environmental factors. In either case, it is not the fault of the young person affected by it. Yelling at him, heaping ridicule on him, punishing him, or in any way making him feel like an inferior being harms him. And it does no good. As parents, we should think of the child's feelings, rather than our own. We should tell him that he should have the services of a psychiatrist, or of any other counselor, to help him evaluate what is going on. We should tell the youngster that his sexual problem may be only part of his over-all difficulties. If he objects to getting help, we should encourage him to do so. We should let him know that we are primarily concerned with his welfare, and that we want to help him in any way we can.

There is one matter related to homosexuality that all of us should discuss with our children, especially during their teens. As stated previously, opinions vary about the normality of this state of being, but, whatever our thoughts concerning homosexuality, we should recognize that society's treatment of the homosexual has been unjust.

Why must we have laws punishing adult human beings for sexual activity carried on in private between consenting adults? This should not be the concern of anyone but the people involved. Otherwise law-abiding citizens should not be subject to restrictive laws concerning their private sexual behavior. If these laws did not exist, for example, there would be no real or imagined justification for dismissing a homosexual person from a job. As with heterosexual activity, there must of course be laws that protect the rights of children.

Most of us have been brought up so that we have some prejudice against homosexuals. Although we do not become afraid that every heterosexual guest in our home will seduce our teen-age daughter, we are apt to fear that a homosexual guest might seduce our adolescent son.

Our teen-age children will be interested in, and influenced by, our opinions. Let us tell them that homosexuals are every bit as human as heterosexuals. Tell them that we disapprove of a society where undercover agents spend time trapping harmless people in washrooms, rather than devoting their energy to fighting serious crime. We should tell our young people that it is wrong to make fun of homosexuals. It is wrong to deny them rights of any kind simply because of their sexual orientation.

Hopefully, society's attitude toward its homosexual members will change. Homosexuals themselves may help with this. Recently, in an election for a nonvoting delegate from the District of Columbia to the House of Representatives, an avowed homosexual candidate campaigned openly. He had no more chance of winning this election than did any of the other minority-party candidates, but he presented his views on the issues with self-assurance and with obvious self-respect. A good omen.

CHAPTER X

Modern Problems: From Pot to TV to Mixed Marriages

Television

"I'd like your advice about something," a well-to-do lady said to the psychiatrist. "I'm getting a new television set and I want to put it in the room of one of our three children. I don't know whose room it should be. What do you think I should do?"

"Buy three television sets," the doctor answered, "and put one in each room."

THE WOMAN involved in this episode looked shocked. "Why, Doctor," she said, "won't I spoil them by doing this?"

If this mother had to deny herself anything in order to follow the doctor's suggestion it would have been terrible advice. However, for a person of her means, buying three television sets merely represented putting an additional piece of furniture in each child's room. As was explained to her, the significant factor would not be the presence of television in each bedroom, but the establishment, on the part of the parents, of proper limits on the use of the sets.

Television is one of the elements in our culture that is blamed for many problems and provokes much anxiety. We wonder what programs children should or should not watch. Should television be allowed on school nights? Does it keep youngsters from doing their homework? Is it good or bad for children?

In one way or another television is a fact of life for all of us and for our offspring. They are exposed to varied aspects of life that in previous times would largely be kept out of their awareness. Television provides them with views of foreign places and peoples, and can familiarize them with distant cultures. It can be a source of knowledge and entertainment and enjoyment; it can go along with other pleasant things in life. But it can also be a means of escaping work and responsibility. Children can become addicted to television for lack of something that would be more fun to do.

In itself television is neither good nor evil, but simply an instrument whose effect depends on what we make of it. As with various aspects of daily living, the attitude of our youngsters toward television largely reflects our own behavior. If they notice that television viewing is our main recreational activity, they may very well follow our example. When they observe that only a small portion of our leisure time is spent in this manner, they too may find other forms of amusement and relaxation.

For years, a number of parents have used television as an electronic baby sitter or pacifier. To a busy mother with several young children, its use in this way can be a godsend. No one would quarrel with something that gives her a brief respite. Nevertheless, we have to be careful to avoid an imbalance where the youngster gets too much stimulation from the tube and not enough from his relationship with a mothering person. For the latter is most important for proper growth and development.

There is much concern with the effect of television on children, and with what rules need to be established in a home pertaining to its use. What should we do about television and what should we tell our offspring about it?

The answers to these questions will vary, depending on the particular child and household. We should be wary of anyone who gives us formula-type answers. For example, in some families television is severely restricted, with no watching done except on weekends. This may work well, especially if the parents adhere to a similar schedule in their own viewing habits. It would be surprising, however, to find many people who set such an example to go along with the prohibitions to their children. In other homes, there is practically no restriction on viewing time, and this too can operate very satisfactorily.

Does television interfere with schoolwork? This is a frequently asked question. In order to attempt an answer we must look at the individual involved. There are students who maintain a straight-*A* average and do all their homework to the constant accompaniment of television. Would any parent be justified in telling this child to turn off the set while he is doing his schoolwork?

On the other hand there are hyperactive youngsters with a short attention span who will be distracted from their work by any sight or sound. It would be almost impossible for them to concentrate on their work with the television blaring. Limits have to be set for these children. They should be told that the reasons for setting the rules is to provide them with the proper atmosphere for doing their lessons.

Our approach to the use of television on school nights should be individualized. Our restrictions on its use will depend on how a specific child is functioning. We need not jump to the conclusion that watching television will always have an adverse effect on school performance.

In general it has been my feeling that we worry too much about the immediate and long-range effects of television viewing on children. Television is with us and there is no way to be rid of it. Even if we keep it out of our home, our children will be exposed to their playmates' recounting of what they have been seeing. Television can be a tremendous educational force in both positive and negative ways.

A child who is progressing satisfactorily in his development probably requires little restriction of his television viewing, other than that it conform to bedtime and similar reasonable expectations of everyday behavior. It has been my observation that children who have had almost unrestricted access to television do not become addicted to it, providing they have been exposed to other forms of recreation and learning. It is ludicrous for a parent to become angry at his child for watching too much television when the same parent has not encouraged him to try other types of recreation. This parent should stimulate varied interests in his child.

Some children censor their own viewing. There are those who enjoy shows dealing with supernatural themes. They have chills going up their spines and enjoy the chills. Others are uncomfortable and fearful of such programs. They may turn off the set or leave the room rather than watch. Certain shows will be avoided for a period of time and then watched again when a child has overcome a particular fear. We should not try to force a youngster to watch what he would prefer to steer clear of, and we should not tease him about any feelings of discomfort.

On the whole, when a child is doing well in his work and in his relationships with his peers, we can leave the quantity of television watching up to him. In any event, rather than restrict television completely, it would be wiser to set a limit on the amount of time we feel can be permitted each day. The child can have the choice of what programs will occupy the allotted interval.

Parents often feel that they must censor certain shows or even parts of programs. Frequently this makes the child more interested in, and fascinated with, the content of the forbidden program. One father stated that his eight-year-old son watched the news with him each evening. But when they were about to show gruesome war pictures he asked the boy to leave the room. It was suggested to this parent that he either not watch the news himself when he came home from work, or, preferably, that he continue to permit his son to watch with him, and then take the time to ask the boy what thoughts and questions he had about what they had seen together.

Too much of the time we have no idea what our children are watching. We then miss the opportunity of discussing with them our views and feelings about what is going on in the world.

Diet and Exercise

On Saturday night the nine-year-old boy would go down to the corner of Sixth Avenue and watch the man in the cowboy hat with his Indian assistant on the stagelike platform of their truck. The man would throw knives, do magic tricks, and then go into his spiel about the medicinal wonders of the white liquid which he was selling for a dollar and would be guaranteed to prolong one's life.

The boy watched in amazement and thought, "I wish I could get some and take it home to my parents."

FORTY YEARS have gone by since I stood on the corner wanting to believe that the bottle of medicine could fulfill all the promises the patent-medicine man was making. But, of course, the claims for the white medicine were a fraud, and it could not prolong anyone's life. We may not have been able to do much about the future health of our parents, but we may be able to tell our children things that will enable them to lead a longer and healthier life.

Increasingly we hear of heart attacks in younger people, particularly males. There is evidence of already-existing changes in the blood vessels of young men who have died of other causes. While there is no unanimous opinion about all of the factors that cause heart attacks, certain things seem significant. Smoking increases the risk. Diet may be important. Heredity and diseases such as diabetes play a part. Emotional stress and lack of physical exercise enter into it.

We cannot do anything about heredity. We can see to it that there is proper treatment for disease. We may or may not be able to minimize the stress of everyday life. But we can teach our children something about smoking, diet, and exercise.

Most of us who pay attention to these things in our own daily habits may be trying to lock the barn door after the horse is gone, but, hopefully, we will forestall the development of a heart attack or at least better our chances of surviving one if it occurs. However, if we can convince our children to pay more attention to these matters, we do them a great favor. We do not want to scare them with the prospect of early heart attacks. We do want to encourage them to develop a way of life that will forestall trouble later.

A teen-age child may ask us why he should not smoke since relatively few people get lung cancer. He should be told that the dangers of trouble with his blood vessels and heart are even more important than lung cancer. Many of us have a problem in talking to our youngsters about smoking because we ourselves have not been able to give it up. We should explain to the child that when we started smoking the dangers that are evident now were not known. The fact that we became addicted and may not be able to stop smoking is all the more reason for them not to start. We can tell them that we realize it is difficult not to take up smoking when many of their peers smoke, but it is a habit that can seriously harm their health.

The establishment of a proper diet in one's household is the best way to tell a child about the importance of the food he eats. Getting a child to think about the right kind of foods to eat will be a problem, for some of the things that should be avoided, such as ice cream, are the very foods that are so enjoyable. But at least in the adolescent years we should explain to our children that a diet containing a lot of the wrong kind of fat is not a healthy one. One type of fat, which is called saturated, may cause a waxy substance, cholesterol, to be deposited in the blood vessels. More of this kind of fat is found in milk (except skim milk), butter, cream, cheese, and meats like pork, beef, and lamb, than in other foods. Other fats, called unsaturated, do not seem to cause the same problems. These are more plentiful in liquid vegetable oils, in fish, and vegetables. We should encourage our children to avoid becoming overweight, and we should tell them that they should attempt to stick to a diet which takes into account some of the factors that now seem important for the prevention of heart disease.

Probably one of the best things we can do for our youngsters is to interest them in regular exercise and to encourage them to keep it up as they get older. Most of us have become more and more sedentary, and too often our youngsters follow our example. For some children, desire to engage in competitive athletics provides sufficient activity. They should be advised to maintain their physical fitness with other forms of exercise during other seasons of the year. We should try to involve them in games such as tennis which provides good workouts and can be continued throughout life.

Some children are very awkward. They may shy away from ball games because of their feeling of inadequacy. We should tell these youngsters that it is not their fault they were born with poor coordination. We can tell them that it is important for their well-being to get regular exercise. We should try to get these children to walk long distances with us or to jog. It will do them good and do us good too. In fact, even the well-coordinated ones should benefit from regular physical training. There will be an added dividend if the activity is one in which fathers and children can all engage. They will be together and can talk before and after the exercise sessions.

We cannot guarantee to prevent heart attacks, but much evidence is accumulating that a prudent diet and a regularly maintained exercise program are of great benefit. We should encourage our children to establish proper habits in these areas so that they do not have to change fixed patterns of living later. If we can do this, we will be giving them a most valuable gift.

Drugs

"Promise us you won't try pot," Mr. Howard said to his son, Chip.
"But I don't think I can promise you that."
"We insist that you promise us," said his mother.
"O.K. I promise," answered Chip.

PARENTS ARE increasingly disturbed by the thought that their children may be using drugs. Chip's parents showed their concern by forcing a halfhearted promise from him.

It is not wise to tell a child he must promise us not to use marijuana. If he is going to experiment with it, we put him in the position of making a dishonest pledge. If he feels he should not use drugs, no oath will be necessary.

Much has been written about drugs and their possible effects. We will not go into these details here, but we will discuss what we might hear from children, and what we can tell them about our own position about drugs.

We should realize that when children use drugs, there will be, in general, several different patterns of behavior. Some youngsters will smoke marijuana on a few occasions out of curiosity, much in the same way most of us tried cigarette smoking in our teens. Other young people will use it with some degree of regularity on weekends, in the same way that their parents drink at cocktail parties. Still others will be heavily involved in smoking pot, and in taking other drugs, to the point where it becomes a major interest.

What should our attitude be if we find that our child has experimented with marijuana? There is a danger of parents becoming too upset in the case of a youngster who has only experimented a little. A child may be taken immediately to the family physician in an attempt to instill fear about the dangers of marijuana into him. Such action is usually not called for and may create unnecessary resentment in him.

It is better if we, ourselves, handle matters with our child. We should tell him that we know young people are curious and want to try things, but we disapprove of this action. It is against the law, and we do not expect our children to break the law. We can tell him that while we understand them wanting to see what drugs are like, we do not want them to continue using them.

Young people will tell us the law is wrong, and since pot is no worse than alcohol, the law should be changed. We should tell them that, even if marijuana is legalized, it is inconceivable that its use would be permitted for those under eighteen years of age. We can tell them they are free to work toward changing the law, but not justified in disregarding it. While many of us may agree that the penalties for possession of pot are too severe, the person who is convicted of this offense will have a police record which can trouble him later in life.

Unfortunately, too many scare stories have been told by certain authorities about the dangers of drugs. Because of their own experience youngsters may react by believing nothing of what they hear, and tell us they believe there is no danger from any drugs. The truth is, we do not know the answers to some of these questions, especially the long-term effects of marijuana use. Research is just in the beginning stages.

We should tell children that even drugs prescribed by physicians sometimes have bad side effects. Some of these effects were not noticed until the drugs had been in use over a long period of time and in many patients. We can explain that it seems foolish to use quantities of illegal drugs which may also be contaminated with other substances. One local university newspaper, for example, ran an advertisement advising its readers not to purchase mescaline because batches of it were adulterated with rat poison.

Occasionally, children will come home and ask their parents to try marijuana with them, using the argument, "How can you be so much against it when you've never even tried it?" Some parents do this, perhaps out of their own curiosity, or because they feel the youngsters may have a point. Such action is a mistake. We may feel that our children may try marijuana, but we should not be in the position of sanctioning its use for them.

We should try to give children a positive reason for not using drugs. Their teen-age years should be a time for putting up with uncomfortable feelings and for trying to find resources within themselves for coping with life's problems, rather than resorting to the artificial comfort provided by drugs. They may inform us that many adults use tranquillizers and alcohol. We may agree with this observation, but we can tell them it does not make sense for young people to disapprove of their elders' behavior, and then copy it by substituting pot for alcohol.

If we find our children using drugs on more than a passing experimental basis, we should take whatever steps we can to discourage this. We should tell them we will not support this habit by giving them money for it. We should have an idea of how much money they are getting and how they are spending it. We should make our disapproval of their actions very clear to them, but also focus our attention on what problems they may be having other than drugs.

Youngsters who become heavily committed to drugs and who apparently have little control over themselves may have to be hospitalized as a first step toward straightening out their difficulties. Parents may mistakenly avoid taking such a step because of embarrassment. A narcotic agent told me of arresting a teen-ager who was using heroin. When the agent saw syringes and needles openly displayed in the boy's bedroom, he asked the parents if they knew what their son had been doing. They said they did, but the boy had promised them he was going to stop soon. We should not believe such promises. In such an instance do not let anything stand in the way of trying to get a child treatment. If he will not accept it voluntarily, we may have to go to the Juvenile Court in our community, and tell them that the child is beyond our control.

Parents of students in the lower grades are worrying about drug problems. Anticipating future difficulties they ask what can they do to prevent their children's exposure to the temptation of drugs. We will not be able to prevent such exposure. The best insurance against this problem is the development of healthy personalities in their youngsters. A child who has adequate interests and sufficient self-esteem may experiment with drugs briefly, but he will not become committed to them as a way of life.

Marriage

Victor and Linda had married when they were both eighteen. Now they were twenty years old and were getting a divorce. Linda was telling a psychiatrist about her husband's faults which she felt made it impossible to live with him.

"Didn't you know he had those habits before you married him?" asked the doctor.

"Yes, I did, but I thought he would change."

A MOST neglected area in the education of our children is the subject of marriage. The establishment and maintenance of a good marriage is one of the more difficult jobs in life. Yet, little careful thought appears to go into the making of this most important decision.

By a good marriage we mean one in which most of the healthy needs of both partners are met. In addition, when a child arrives, neither parent should have to look upon the baby as a competitor.

I have given considerable thought over a long period of time to the question of how we can tell and teach our children about the importance of their decisions related to marriage. I am not always optimistic that this can be successfully accomplished. Generally, when one is full of love and infatuation he is not going to stop and think of the practical realities of having to live with another person for many years. Yet, as parents it is our duty to get our children to stop and think about this subject.

If our teen-age children come to us and say they are in love and want to get married, we should tell them to give a great deal of serious thought to this decision. We need to tell them that, while physical attraction is important, they also need to consider matters that will be of significance later. Have the two young people compared their views on sex, money, religion, politics, child rearing, relatives, occupations, recreation, and responsibility? If they have not gone into these matters, we should tell them to do so before they make a final decision.

Our child may come to us and say he wants to marry someone of another race or religion. First, what should we *not* say to him? I do not believe that we should tell him not to do this simply because we object to such a marriage. We should not tell him he will be hurting us by doing this. We should not tell him he is wrong for wanting to do this. In truth, he may be right in the feeling that religion (or race) should make no difference among people.

Then what should we tell him? We should tell him that marriage is a complicated business. It is not easy for two individuals to live together and depend on each other and manage the stresses of life. We can add that this process becomes even more difficult when there are marked differences in background and outlook between the marital partners. We should also tell him that while there may or may not be problems for a couple in a mixed marriage, the situation becomes much more complex when they have children. We should tell him to consider the step he plans to take from these standpoints. We can make the point that, because of society's attitudes, a mixed marriage requires two people of more than average maturity to make it work. He should honestly try to consider if he and his intended wife have this degree of maturity.

Occasionally, a child may have an attitude similar to Linda's, the girl who was quoted at the start of this discussion. She may say, "Yes, there are a few things about him I don't like but I know he will change or I will change him." We should tell her that if she doesn't feel she can live with him as he is, she should not marry him. Husbands and wives can change during the course of a marriage, but young people should not marry if they feel one of them will have to change if they are to make a go of it.

As a child grows up in a family, he learns about marriage by what he observes about his parents. Are they happy with each other most of the time? Are they considerate of each other? Can they at times criticize one another constructively and still be loving and devoted to one another and to their children?

Certainly, in terms of the enjoyment of life a good marriage is every bit as important to our children as the choice of a college and a career. We should impress this on our children, particularly on our teen-age children, and encourage them to give serious thought to this matter.

Religion

"In spite of our different religions we decided to get married and have gotten along pretty well. We haven't given our ten-year-old son, Tom, any religious instruction. We felt it would be more fair if he could choose for himself when he got older."

BECAUSE OF their religious differences, these parents waited many years before they married. Neither one converted and neither expected the other to do so. They did have difficulty in deciding how their child should be taught, however, and they avoided a decision by assuming it could be left up to him to decide when he became an adolescent.

Several things are wrong with this approach. First, the young man will have no basis on which to make a choice. A child who is given an education in the principles of a particular religion will accept or reject its teachings when he becomes an adult, but his decision will be based on some knowledge of his religion. Second, Tom may feel disloyal to one parent if he chooses to be associated with the religious group of the other parent. Third, he may not know how to answer when a classmate asks, "What are you?" referring to religion.

For the children's sake, partners in a mixed-religion marriage should make a definite determination of how their offspring will be raised. If the preschool child asks, "What religion are we?" he should be answered in a definite way, based on the parents' decision. A child who is already attending Sunday school may ask why he is going to Mother's church rather than Father's. He can be told that the important parts of religion, which have to do with behaving decently, can be learned in any church. He can also be told that, since Mother and Father were brought up in different ways, they had to decide which one he would attend and they both decided where he would go. As with many aspects of parent-child relationships, whether or not the youngster accepts what he is told about his parents' difference of religions will depend on the stability of the marriage.

Parents, in general, have questions about religion. They ask if it is all right for them to tell their children to go to church. Before I answer, I want to know if the parents themselves go to church or synagogue fairly regularly. If they do, there is no reason why they should not tell their youngsters either to accompany them or to attend Sunday school while they are in church. This is especially true where pre-adolescent children are concerned.

With adolescents, it is probably wiser to leave the choice up to them. At this age youngsters question what they have been taught about many subjects, and we should permit them to question and doubt religious tenets. If they have had adequate training in their religion, they should be going to church for positive reasons and not because we tell them to. Their non-attendance may be simply a part of adolescent rebellion; we should understand this and tell them that going or not going to church is up to them.

When it comes to religion, we certainly tell our children more by our example than by our words. A child quickly becomes skeptical of what he has been told about the moral and ethical values of his religion if he sees his father praying on the Sabbath and cheating people during the week. If we want a child to share our faith, we must see that *we* really believe in it and do our best to live by its teachings.

Parents should tell children about their religious beliefs. A child needs to know this for purposes of his own identity. If parents are confirmed atheists, their child will be better off if they tell him that this is what they believe and what they want him to believe. Too often, a youngster finds himself attending Sunday school when he knows that his parents are not really a part of any religious group.

We should tell our children that each person has a right to his own religious beliefs. The ethical and moral values of most religions are good ones. We should tell them that religion can be a great comfort to people who have faith in it. We should add that, if we want the privilege of practicing our own religion, we should allow others to differ with us.

Let our children see that we are practitioners of our faith, whatever faith it is, rather than mere purveyors of it.

Prejudice

Peter came home from school very upset.
"What's the matter, Pete?" his mother asked.
"Mom," he said, "a kid called me a dirty nigger today. Why don't people like us?"
"Well, let me see," Mother began. "Some of them think all black people are lazy and don't want to work, and some think we're all on welfare, and . . ."

AN EPISODE like this could occur to any child of a minority group. Peter's mother was not sure how to answer her son. She tried to list reasons that people might give for their dislike of black people.

Prejudice is a condition we all share. If we examine ourselves closely enough, we can all discover areas where we have unreasonable biases. Some of us will at least admit that we are unjustifiably intolerant of certain ideas or of groups of people. We may justify our bigotry by rationalizations: "If God wanted everybody to be the same, he would have made them all the same color." Or we may fall back on stereotypes: "Blacks are shiftless," "Jews are money grubbers," "Catholics are intolerant," "The Irish are drunks."

Children who are members of a racial or religious minority group have to condition themselves to the intolerance of others. Sooner or later they will be exposed to taunts or unfair comments about the group to which they belong. Black youngsters growing up in the city learn quickly that there are people who regard them as inferior because of their color. A few Jewish children living in a predominantly Christian neighborhood may be rejected by their peers because of their religion. And so on.

In our initial example above, Peter's mother should have answered him differently. She should have told him that nothing is wrong with him for being black, but something is wrong with people who dislike you just because you are black. This should be stated quite simply, without any explanation that implies some basis for the prejudiced person's opinion. We should tell our children that a person of any color or religion can be good or bad, fair or unfair, honest or dishonest, lazy or ambitious, and mean or kind. It depends on his particular makeup.

We should tell our youngsters that even though most of us have some prejudices, we should try to understand that there is no real basis for them. Prejudice is not based on knowledge of what a person really is like. We should answer questions in a manner that will maintain the child's self-respect rather than permit him to develop feelings of inferiority because of his religion or race. We can tell him that a prejudiced person is insecure about his own worth and needs to feel that others are inferior to him because of superficial things.

Toy Guns

Five-year-old Larry pointed a water pistol at his playmate and yelled, "Bang, you're dead!"

His mother heard him and called out, "Larry, come in here. I've told you it's not right to play with guns."

Is THIS what we should tell our children about playing with toy guns? Parents have recently become quite concerned with this question because of the increase in violence we are always hearing about. Quite a number of parents have prohibited their youngsters from owning toy guns. Will such play encourage youngsters to be hostile and violent?

It is my opinion that, as long as children know that it is play they are engaged in, the use of toy pistols will not have an adverse effect on them. Depriving children of toy guns does not take away their imagination. They will often make a gun out of clothespins, or the branch of a tree, or simply by extending an index finger in a forward direction with the thumb perpendicular to it and the other three fingers bent back as if gripping a pistol.

I do not believe that the make-believe shooting in itself leads youngsters to feel that violence is an acceptable way of handling problems. I have seen many adolescents who dislike violence and are extremely law abiding, yet, as children, they spent many enjoyable days chasing each other in games of cops and robbers or cowboys and Indians.

Actually, this type of play allows children to work out conflicts and ventilate some of their aggressive urges. As they get older, they will hopefully be helped by their parents to channel these aggressive impulses into more useful outlets, such as competitive sports or responsible political action. Children's attitudes concerning violence come from their observations of our methods of handling anger, rather than from toy-gun play.

We should tell our preschool and lower-grade children that they can play with toy guns providing that they do not try to hurt themselves or their playmates. They are to remember that this is make-believe.

We should not be worried about this type of play if our child seems to be doing well in other aspects of his everyday life. We must be concerned about how he is handling his impulses if he acts in a cruel fashion toward animals or other children. For instance, a child who tortures a cat or dog or who bullies younger children needs help. Parents should then be especially aware that such a child is having particular problems in handling his hostile impulses. It would be well for them to look carefully at how they are handling their own feelings.

A PARTING THOUGHT

As I suggested in the preface, no one can tell parents exactly what words to use in every situation that arises with their children. We cannot anticipate all the varied concerns and questions that our children will have.

However, I have tried to present some of the possible problems that can occur in the lives of parents and their offspring. I hope that parents will be able to reflect on, and utilize, some of the concepts they have acquired by reading this book.

We should give our youngsters truthful information and honest answers. To help them develop into adequate human beings, we should treat them with kindness, firmness, and consistency.

There are unpleasant experiences in life for all of us. There are also times of happiness. Children, with the support of their parents, must learn to cope with adversity and, hopefully, they will also learn to enjoy the pleasures of life.

As parents, we should continue to observe our youngsters and learn with them and from them. Thus we will help them prepare for life in these times of accelerated communication and rapid change. We should remember that our greatest gift to our children is to give them the ability to stand on their own two feet so that they no longer need us.

INDEX

Abandonment, 60, 80
  adopted child's fear of, 148, 153–154
  children of divorced parents fear of, 184
  fears of, 131–133
Abcesses, 68
Abortion, 105, 219
Absent parents. *See* Divorce
Abusive parents, 135–136
Accidents, 71–72, 133
  emotional reactions to, 76–78
  as explanation for suicide, 142
Acting-out, 59, 243
Actions, child's responsibility for, 33, 35, 94, 199–200, 217
Active babies, 20
Adenoidectomy, 67–69
Adenoids, explained, 67
Adopted child. *See* Adoption
Adoption, 146–157
  abondonment fears in, 153–154
  anger of child in, 151–153
  explaining conception to child of, 149–151
  environment and, 155–157
  heredity and, 155–157
  natural parents and, 147, 148, 150, 154
  secrecy in, 149
  special treatment and, 152
  telling child of, 146–149
Adoption agencies, 147
Adolescents. *See* Teen-agers
Adult roles, children playing, 138–140, 187
Affluence, 29–31
Alcohol, 233, 234, 235
Allergies, 58

Amputees, 106, 111–112
Anesthesia for children, 57
Anger:
  at abusive parent, 135
  after accidents, 76–78
  of adopted child, 151–153
  after a death, 127–128, 134, 136–138
  toward divorced parents, 168, 182
  within family, 31–34
  of handicapped children, 108
  at losing games, 173–174
  after permanent loss of function, 75
  toward psychiatric treatment, 53
  of stepchild, 194–196, 200–201
  at teachers, 96, 101–102
Animals, fear of, 64
Antisocial behavior, 183
Anxiety, 24, 61, 79, 153
Appendicitis, 62
Athletic ability, 120, 173
Athletics, 71
Attentiveness to child, parental, 23, 30
Attitudes, parental, toward:
  adoption, 146, 149–151, 157
  affluence, 30
  child rearing, 18
  children after divorce, 175–177
  children's misbehavior after divorce, 184
  death, 125
  delinquency, 42
  divorce, 160–161
  drugs, 233–235
  education, 87, 88
  ex-mates, 181–182
  fatally ill child, 83–84

grades, 91–92
handicapped children, 104–106
homosexuality, 223
personal problems, 15
psychiatry, 53
retarded child, 114
religion, 240
responsibility as stepparents, 196
school failure, 94
sex, 170–171, 208, 211, 218
spouse after divorce, 166–167
stepchildren, 194–195
suicide, 143
teachers, 97
television, 227
toy guns, 242–243
Authority, 34–35
   respect for, 96
Automobile driving, 42
Awkwardness, 119, 120, 220, 232

Baby-sitters, 191, 225
Bad dreams. *See* Nightmares
Behavior, changes in, 65, 137, 141, 182–183
Bickering, 33, 53, 160, 190, 204
Bigotry. *See* Prejudice
Birth defects, 104–105, 108, 110
Blame, parental, 18–21
   handicapped children and, 105
Bleeding, 68, 73
Bodily harm, fear of, 63–67
"Booster shots," 48
Boys' clubs, 182
Brain damage, 110
   mild, 20
Brain dysfunction, minimal, 115–119
Brain wave test, 48
Breast enlargement, in adolescent boys, 214
Broken bones, 71–75
Broken homes. *See* Divorce
Burial:
   explaining, 124–128
   and funerals, 126–128
   misconceptions concerning, 126
   see also Death
Business, 23, 43

Callus, 73
Casts, plaster, 71–75
Censorship, 229

Child custody, 165, 179, 187, 198
   holidays and, 204
Childlessness, 23
   see also Adoption
Child psychiatrists, 53–54
Children, adopted. *See* Adoption
Children, comparisons between, 19, 95, 110
Children's Hospital of the District of Columbia, 57, 59
Churchgoing, 239–240
Cigarette smoking. *See* Smoking
Circumcision, 66
Closeness, 27, 114, 139, 186
College entrance, 86–89
Comminuted fracture, 72
Compensation, 20, 30, 108, 118
Competition with stepparent, 200–201
Complete fractures, 72
Compound fractures, 72
Compromise, 36
Conception, adopted child and, 149–151
   see also Sex
Condolences, 140
Conduct, moral, 40–43, 218–219
Consistency, 148
   of children of divorce, 190
   divorced parents and, 174–175
   in family problems, 35–37
   hyperactive child and, 118
   parental, 35–37
Constitutional differences of children, 20, 94, 156
Contagious disease, 84
Contraceptives, 214–219
Crying, 130
   reasons for, 78, 128–129
Cuddling, 27
Curiosity, 13, 209, 216–217
Custody. *See* Child custody

Dark, fear of, 65
Dating:
   divorced parents and, 171, 190
   widows and, 199
Death, 63, 124–143
   abandonment fears and, 131–133
   of abusive parents, 135–136
   anger over, 136–138
   of children, 129

Index

children's role after, 138–140
disguised unhappiness in, 140–141
explaining, 124–126
and funerals, 126–128
grief over, 128–131
guilt over, 133–135
misconceptions concerning, 124–125, 126
religion and, 125
remarriage after, 198–199
by suicide, 142–143
Defects. *See* Handicapped children
Delinquency, 42–43
Democracy, family as a, 34
Dependency, 109, 131
handicapped children and, 108
Depression, 76–77, 82–83, 124, 130, 143, 183
Desertion, 24
Diabetes, 84, 230
Diet, 230–232
Discipline, 21, 38, 114
divorced parents and, 175, 178, 189–190
stepparents and, 196
Discrimination. *See* Prejudice
Dislocations, 73
Divorce, 160–191
asking children's advice on, 164
child custody in, 164–165
children in middle on, 175–177
children as confidantes in, 164–165, 187–189
constancy of visitation after, 167–172
friendliness of parents after, 166–167
grandparents and, 189–191
meaningful visits for children of, 167–172
reconciliation after, 167
security needs after, 182–185
sexual behavior with children of, 170–171, 185–187
telling children about, 161–164
truthfulness about, 179–180
vindictiveness in, 180–181
winning and losing with child of, 172–175
see also Remarriage
Doctors, 46–84
explanations by, 46–47, 48–51, 55–56, 75
feelings of guilt, 82
medical language and, 54–56
psychiatrists, 51–54
visits to, 47–49
Drugs, 29, 233–236
Dying, fear of, 83, 125, 129

Eating habits, 65
see also Diet
Economic conditions of family, 19–20
Education, 21, 86–102
colleges, 86–89
grades, payment for, 89–92
of handicapped, 111–113
lifelong, 13, 86–87
options to fail in, 92–95
parents and, 87–89
physical defects and, 90
school phobia and, 98–102
special classes, 118
teachers and, 95–98
effect of television on, 228
see also Sex, elementary education in
Elective surgery, 59, 62–63, 79
Electrocardiogram, 50
Electroencephalogram, 48, 50
Emmissions, nocturnal, 213
Emotions, 31–34, 128
see also Anger, Fears, Grief, Guilt
Environment, 14, 19
adopted child and, 155–157
homosexuality and, 220, 223
of hyperactive child, 118
for study, 91
Exercise, 75, 232
Experiences:
new, 24, 108
unpleasant, 15, 56–57, 127
Experimentation, sexual, 215, 222

Failure, allowing for, 92–95
Family problems, 18–43
affluence and, 29–31
authority in, 34–35
consistency and, 35–37
emotions and, 31–34
father's job in, 22–25
morality and, 40–43
mother's job in, 26–31

parental blame in, 18–20
physical punishment for, 37–40
Fatally ill child, 81–84
Fathers, 26–27, 28, 34–35, 60, 63
　absent, 172–174, 182, 196
　homosexuality and, 219–224
　hospitalization of, 78–81
　as role models, 22–25
　stepfathers as, 196
Fears:
　abandonment, 80, 131–133, 148, 153, 184
　accidents, 72
　animals, 64
　bodily harm, 39, 50, 63–67, 70–71, 110
　dark, 65
　dying, 83, 125, 129
　emotional reaction to injury, 76–78
　harm during sleep, 65
　homosexuality, 221
　hospitals, 46–47
　leaving home, 60, 65
　normal, 39, 49, 62
　objects, 63, 64
　operations, 59
　persistent, 65
　physical checkup, 46
　physical punishment, 38
　school, 98–102
　separation, 154
　separation from mother, 62–63, 99, 131
　sexual, 212
　sleeping alone, 139
　strangers, 62–63
　toward the handicapped, 112–113
　toward teachers, 97–98
　visits to the doctor, 47–49
　younger children, 63–67
　see also Nightmares
Feelings *vs* actions, 32–33, 100, 110, 133–135, 162–163, 194, 195–196
Feminine roles, 26–31
Firmness, 36
Food poisoning, 56
Fractures, 47, 71–75
　comminuted, 72
　complete, 72
　compound, 72
　explained, 72

greenstick, 72
healing of, 73
incomplete, 72
reduction of, 73
simple, 72
Freedom, 23, 32
Frustration, feelings of, 32, 126
Funerals, 124, 126–128
　see also Burial, Death

Genetic counseling, 106, 108
Genitalia, 64–65, 70
German measles, 108
Gifted children, 91
Gonorrhea, 217
Grades, 30, 88
　payment for, 89–92
Grandparents, 117, 182, 189–191
Greenstick fractures, 72
Grief, 82–83, 127, 128–131, 188
　sharing, 131
Grieve, right to, 105
Guilt:
　abusive parent and child's, 136
　after a death, 130, 133–135
　of children of divorce, 186
　of divorced parents, 168, 172–173
　doctor's feeling of, 82
　concerning handicapped child, 106
　of handicapped children, 105
　hostility toward parents, 18
　legitimate, 41
　parental, 83
　after parents' divorce, 161–162, 183
　about parent's illness, 79
　over retardation, 114
　sibling rivalry, 34
Guns, toy, 242–243

Half-siblings, 202–203
Handicapped children, 104–121
　brain dysfunction, minimal, of, 115–119
　child's feeling toward, 106–109
　hyperactivity of, 115–119
　mild handicaps of, 119–121
　parent's feeling toward, 104–106
　and retardation, 113–115
　school problems of, 111–113
　sibling's feeling toward, 109–111
Handicaps:

after injury, 75
explaining to child, 107
Heart attacks, 230, 232
Height problems, 120
Hematomas, 73
Hereditary illness, 84, 108, 143, 230–231
Hereditary:
  adopted child and, 155–157
  environmental influences and, 155–156
  homosexuality and, 223
Hernia, explained, 69
Hernia repair, 47, 66, 69–71
Heroin, 235
Holidays, sharing, 204
Homework, 90–91, 93, 95, 226
  television and, 226, 228
Homosexuality, 219–224
Honesty, 41, 43
Hospitalization, in drug addiction, 235–236
Hospitals, 46–84
  elective surgery and, 62–63
  emotional reactions to, 76–78
  fatally ill child in, 81–84
  going to, 56–59
  parents at, 60–61
  parents as patients in, 78–81
  personnel of, 61, 77, 78, 82
  preparations for, 58
  routine in, 57–59
  visiting hours of, 60
  younger children and, 63–67
Hostile feelings. *See* Anger
Household chores, 26
Hyperactivity, 94, 115–119, 141
  television and, 228
Hyperkinesis. *See* Hyperactivity
Hypersensitivity, 20
Hypochondria, 64

Identity, sexual, 220, 222
Illegitimacy, 150
Illness, 21, 54, 63
  fatal, 81–84
  hereditary, 84, 108, 142
  of a parent, 79
  school fears and, 99
  see also Hospitals, Operations
Immobilization, 74, 77

Immunization injections, 48, 50
Inadequacy, feelings of, 18–19
Incomplete fractures, 72
Independence, 131
Infancy, 13, 20, 27, 32, 62, 86, 131
  signs of retardation in, 113
Infatuation, 237
Infection, 68
Inguinal hernia. *See* Hernia repair
Initiative, 31
Injuries, 24–25, 71–75
  emotional reactions to, 76–78
Injustice, 30
Insecurity, parental, 19
Institutionalization, 113, 115
Instruments, medical, 47–50
Intellectual endowment, 91
Intercourse, sexual, 211, 212, 216, 218
Interpersonal relationships, 54
  see also Family problems
Intoxication, 172
Intravenous injections, 58

Jealousy:
  half-sibling and, 203
  sibling rivalry, 84, 165
  toward stepparent, 200
Jogging, 242
Joyriding, 42

Kindergarten, 86
Kindness, 36, 148

Language, medical, 54–56
Law, 35, 42
  divorce and, 178–179
  drugs and, 234
  homosexuals and, 223
Leaving home, fear of, 65
Legalistic arguments, 34
Lesbians. *See* Homosexuality
Limitations on behavior, 14, 34, 35, 38
  divorced parents and, 174
  see also Rules
Listening, 14–15
Living arrangements after divorce, 164–165, 190
Loneliness, 185, 187, 200
Loss of function, 75
Love, 33–34, 114, 148, 174

competition with stepparent and, 200
stepchildren and, 197
teen-agers in, 237
Loyalty, divided, 164, 175–176, 195, 198, 239
Lung cancer, 231
Luxuries. *See* Affluence
Lying, 43

Manliness, 216, 220
Marijuana, 233
Marriage, 236–238
Masturbation, 213–214, 215
Material possessions. *See* Affluence
Maturity of divorced parents, 176
Medical examinations, specialized, 48–50, 117
Medication for hyperactivity, 117, 118
Mental health clinics, 102, 141
Menstruation, 212–213
Mescaline, 234
Middle-class youngsters, 29, 42
Middle-ear infections, 68
Mildly handicapped child, 119–121
Minority groups, 241–242
Misconceptions, 15, 47
　of adopted child, 153
　concerning diagnoses, 56
　concerning doctors, 50
　about marriage, 171
　about operations, 59
　about sex, 209–210, 211
　of younger children, 65
Mixed marriages, 237–240
Modern problems, 226–244
　alcohol, 233, 234, 235
　diet, 230–232
　drugs, 233–236
　exercise, 232
　guns, toy, 242–243
　illness, 230–232
　marriage, 236–238
　mixed marriages, 237–240
　prejudice, 241–242
　religion and, 238–240
　smoking, 230–231
　television, 226–229
　violence, 242–243
Money, 23, 30–31, 41, 43, 173, 235
Mongolism, 113
Moral teaching, 40–43
Mothers, 26–31, 35, 60
　homosexuality and, 221
　hospitalization of, 78–81
　as role models, 26–31
　stepmothers as, 194
Movies, 126, 128

Neglect, 22, 24, 109
　of children of divorce, 182, 203
Neighborhood, 21
Nervous system abnormality, minimal, 20
Neurological examination, 117
New baby, 63, 80
　handicapped, 110
New freedom in sex, 214–219
Nightmares, 63, 139–140, 183
Nudity, 185–186, 209
Nursery school, 87

Objects, fear of, 63
Older children, 60–61
　see also Teen-agers
Operating rooms, 57–59
Operations, 46–84
　adenoidectomy, 67–69
　emotional reactions to, 76–78
　explanations of, 66–67
　fractures, 71
　hernia repair, 66, 69–71
　parents', 80
　tonsillectomy, 67–69

Parents:
　abusive, 135
　adoptive, 146–157
　attraction of child to, 183
　blame in family problems, 18–21
　death of both, 132–133
　as educators, 86–87
　exploited by children, 36–37
　fatal illness of, 80
　friendship after divorce of, 166–167
　hospitalization of, 78–81
　hostility toward, 79, 93–94, 100, 133–134, 162
　hostility toward divorced, 183
　hostility toward stepparents, 194
　margin for error, 19
　perfect, 18

see also Attitudes, parental
Passive babies, 20
Peers, 13, 21, 22, 39, 88, 102, 137, 156, 173, 222
Perfection, 18
Permissiveness, 36, 38
Personality development, 14, 25, 30, 62
  adversity and, 78
Phenobarbital, 117
Physical checkup, 46, 47–49
Physiotherapy, 74
"Pill," the, 214–219
Postoperative care, 69, 71
Poverty, 30
Pregnancy, teen-age, 212, 214–219
Prejudice, 97, 237
Preschool years, 27
Pressures for college entrance, 87–88
Priorities, conflicting, 22
Privacy, 186
Psychiatrists, 102, 137, 141
  child, 53–54
  children of divorce and, 178
  homosexuality and, 223
Psychiatry, 51–54
Puberty, 211–214
  see also Teen-agers
"Pumping" children, 177
Punishment:
  hyperactive child and, 117
  illness as a, 77, 83
  physical, 37–40, 100, 135–136
  types of, 39

Race. *See* Prejudice
Rationalizations, 41
Reconciliations, 160, 167
Recovery rooms, 58
"Reducible" hernia. *See* Hernia repair
"Rejecting mother," 20
Relatives, 81, 117, 124, 137, 140, 142, 182
Religion, 125, 137, 208, 239–240
Remarriage, 171, 177, 194–205
  anger of stepchild in, 194–196
  assuming parental responsibility in, 196–197
  competition with stepparents in, 200–202
  deciding on, 198–200

  half-siblings of, 202–203
  mixed feelings about, 198, 200
  need for security and, 204–205
  special occasions and, 204
Respect, mutual, 32
Retardation, 27, 105, 110
Revolution, sexual. *See* Sex
Rights of others, 30, 41
Rigidity, 36
Role models, parents as, 25, 41, 170, 181, 221
Rooming-in, 60, 63
Routine, hospital, 57–59
Rules, 14, 34–35, 39
  divorced parents and, 175, 177–178, 189–190
  schoolwork, 91
  for television viewing, 228
Rural environment, 23

Scars, 71
School personnel, 50, 113
School phobia, 98–102
School problems, 111–113
  see also Education
Schoolwork. *See* Education
Secrecy:
  divorced parents and, 176
  about sex, 215
Security, need for, 182
Sedatives, 117
Seduction, 223–224
Seductiveness, 186
Self-discipline, 38–39
Self-esteem, 23, 31, 91, 102
  of adopted child, 148, 150
  of children of divorce, 181
  drug use and, 235
  of handicapped children, 108, 120
  of hyperactive children, 117
  prejudice and, 242
Sentiment, 34
Separation, 160–191
  see also Divorce
"Separation anxiety," 60, 99, 131
Sex, 208–224
  adolescent development and, 211–214
  attitudes of parents toward, 208–211, 218
  attraction of child to parent of opposite, 162

biological explanations, 209–211
curiosity about, 209, 216–217
elementary education in, 208–211
emissions, 213
experimentation, 215, 222
fears concerning, 212, 217, 221
homosexuality, 219–224
impulses toward children, 185–187
masturbation, 213–214, 215
menstruation, 212–213
misconceptions about, 208–211
new freedom in, 214–219
religious beliefs and, 208
telling adopted child about, 149–151
truthfulness concerning, 209, 210–211
younger children and, 209
see also Pregnancy, teen-age
Sexual fantasies, 186, 214
Shame, 81
Siblings, 19–20, 33, 39, 63, 156
"bossed" by older children, 139
explaining divorce to, 163
fatally ill child and, 84
feelings, 109–111
grades and, 91
half-siblings, 202–203
handicapped child's, 109
retarded child's, 114
rivalry of, 84, 165
school and, 95–96
separation of, in divorce cases, 165
Simple fracture, 72
Sleep, fear of harm during, 65
Slow development, 113
Smoking, 232
Socioeconomic conditions, 21
Spankings. See Punishment, physical
Special privileges, 110
Speech problems, 119, 121
Status, college as a symbol of, 87–88
Stepchildren. See Remarriage
Stepparents. See Remarriage
Stereotypes, 242
Stimulant drugs, 117
Stitches. See Sutures
Strangers, fear of, 62–63
"Strangulated" hernia. See Hernia repair
Student unrest, 29

Subcultures, 21
Substitute mothers, 27
Suicide, 142–143
Support, parental, 25, 35
awkward child and, 221
fatally ill child and, 82–84
of handicapped children, 108
Surgery. See Elective surgery, Operations
Surrogate parents, 132, 154, 185
Sutures, 66
Swollen glands, 68
Symptons, 141, 183
Syphilis, 217

Tactile stimulation, 27
Teachers, 90, 95–98, 156
handicapped children and, 112–113
of hyperactive children, 118
respect for, 96
school problems and, 101
Technology, 23
Teen-agers, 22, 32, 64, 76
adopted, 147
assuming adult role, 188
diet and, 231
divorce and, 184
drugs and, 233–235
exercise and, 232
handicapped, 108
homosexuality and, 222–223
hyperactivity in, 119
marriage and, 237–238
new sexual freedom and, 214–215
effect of parent's death on, 141
pregnancy and, 212, 214–219
religion and, 240
remarriage and, 198–199
retarded, 115
school problems and, 102
sex and, 211–214
sexual behavior of parents toward, 186
smoking and, 231
surrogate parents for, 133
Television, 48, 91, 95, 215, 226–229
Tenderness, 128
Terminal illness. See Fatally ill child
Terminology, medical. See Language, medical
Testing, 87

Index

Tests, medical, 48–50
Thalidomide, 105
Therapy, 33
    and abortion, 219
    for adopted child, 219
    fatally ill child and, 84
    for handicapped children, 107
    speech, 121
    see also Physiotherapy, Psychiatry
Threats, 40, 154
"Throwing" games, 173
Tics, 65, 141
Timidity, 65
Toilet habits, 65, 141, 183
Tonsils, explained, 67–68
Tonsillectomy, 47, 66, 67–69
Tours, hospital, 59
Toys, 59
    guns as, 242–243
Traction, 72, 74, 76
Tradition, 26
Tranquillizers, 235
Truancy, 99
Truthfulness, 15, 56–57, 58, 125, 129, 142, 150, 173, 209, 234

Unhappiness, disguised, 140–141
United front, 36

Values, 41, 87, 170
Vandalism, 42
Venereal disease, 217
Vindictiveness, 180–181
Violence, 39, 242–243
Virginity, 216
Visitation days, meaningful, 167–172, 174, 179, 203, 204
Visits to hospital, 60–61, 77, 80

Wealth. *See* Affluence
"Wet dreams," 213
Whippings. *See* Punishment, physical
Working mothers, 28, 189, 191

X-rays, 48–50, 73

Younger children, 39, 54, 60, 77, 80
    adopted, 147
    divorce and, 180
    fears of, 63–67
    hyperactivity in, 115–119
    mixed marriages and, 239
    effects of parents' death on, 141
    religion and, 239–240
    school fears of, 99
    sex and, 209

FUNDERBURG LIBRARY

MANCHESTER COLLEGE

649.1
OL8w